Creating
Family
Newsletters

123 ideas for sharing
memorable moments
with family and friends

❦ ❦ ❦

Also by Elaine Floyd:

Marketing With Newsletters
(Newsletter Resources)

The Newsletter Editor's Handbook
(Newsletter Resources, co-authored with Marvin Arth and Helen Ashmore)

Making Money Writing Newsletters
(Newsletter Resources)

Marketing Your Bookstore with a Newsletter
(Newsletter Resources)

The Newsletter Sourcebook
(North Light Books, co-authored with Mark Beach)

Advertising From the Desktop
(Ventana Press)

Quick and Easy Newsletters
(Newsletter Resources)

Cover and inside pages:
Photography and design:
  VIP Graphics
  St. Louis, MO
  (314) 535-1117

Creating Family Newsletters: 123 ideas for sharing memorable moments with family and friends.

Library of Congress Cataloging-in-Publication Data
Floyd, Elaine, 1961-
Creating family newsletters: 123 ideas for sharing memorable moments with family and friends / Elaine Floyd.— 1st Ed.
        p.   cm.
Includes bibliographical references and index.
ISBN: 0-9630222-7-X

  1. Newsletters.   2. Communication in the family.
3. Electronic newsletters.   4. Genealogical literature-—Publishing—United States.   I. Title.

PN4784.N5F56 1998   646.78
                                     QBI98-824

First Edition. Printed and bound in the United States of America.

Production Team
Editorial manager: Susan Todd
Proofreading: M.T.

Newsletter Resources
(314) 647-0400; fax (314) 647-1609;
http://www.newsletterinfo.com

Distributed to the trade by:
Writer's Digest Books
an imprint of F&W Publications
1507 Dana Ave., Cincinnati, OH 45207
(800) 289-0963; fax: (513) 531-4082

1965 *(L to R):* David, Raymond, Elaine, Deborah and Laura with Nicky, the cat, and Frisky, the dog diplomat who tactfully sized her litter to five.

Dedication:

To my siblings:
Deborah, Laura,
David (in memory)
and Raymond.

I wish we shared
the same ZIP code.

Contents

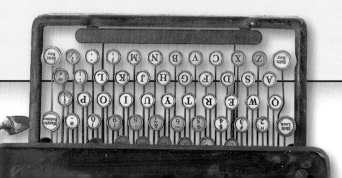

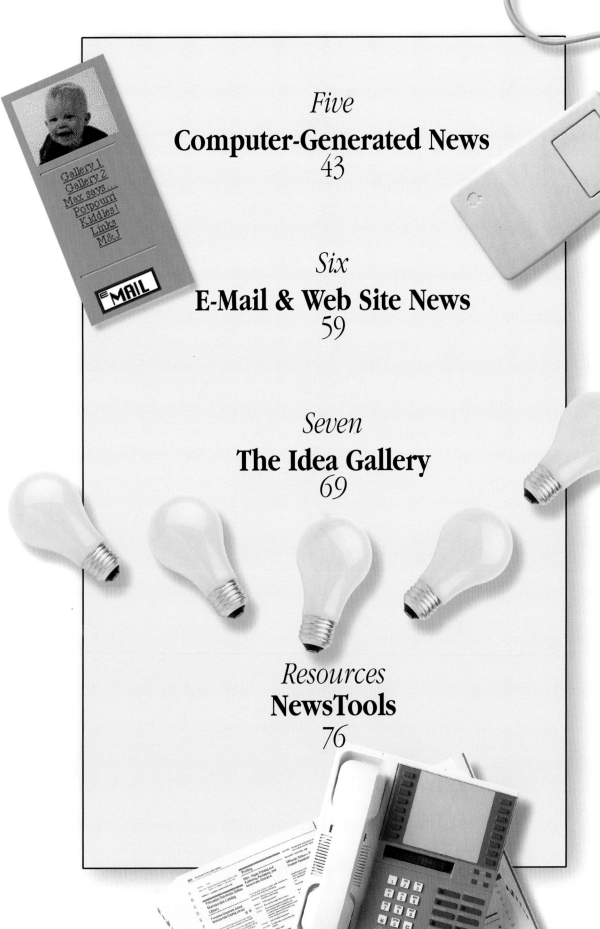

(above) The first issue of *It's All Relative* was "born" when Lisa was on maternity leave with her son. She drew the nameplate with a black marker and created the text on a word processor.

(below) Redesigned with the help of desktop publishing.

An In-Print Get-Together

Over 30 households from three generations and 10 states are getting together every other month in *It's All Relative*. The family is continuing the traditions set by their grandparents (Nana and Pop-Pop) for celebrating their successes and love for life.

The current design with new nameplate type and the removal of what Lisa's brother called "the stick people."

Introduction:
It's All Relative

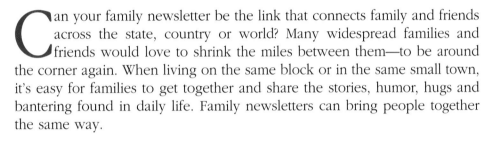

C an your family newsletter be the link that connects family and friends across the state, country or world? Many widespread families and friends would love to shrink the miles between them—to be around the corner again. When living on the same block or in the same small town, it's easy for families to get together and share the stories, humor, hugs and bantering found in daily life. Family newsletters can bring people together the same way.

Creating a "Community" Through News

Graphic designer Lisa Suarez Johnson has created an in-print get-together for her extended family, a newsletter called *It's All Relative*. "Six years ago, my brother approached me about typing up a family newsletter," Lisa explains. "We had been discussing the possibility of a family reunion and he thought it would be a great way to get reacquainted with relatives before the reunion. We asked family members to submit articles for publication, the response was favorable and our family newsletter was born."

It's All Relative is filled with family updates, photos, birth announcements, wedding announcements, vacation news, birthdays, puzzles, recipes, inspirational quotes, jokes, and anything else her readers submit. "In a normal month, I wouldn't get letters from 10 people," says Lisa. "But when it's deadline time, my mailbox is filled."

The newsletter has also brought together all of the family's branches. "Before the newsletter, I wouldn't have even thought to go see a distant cousin in New York," says Lisa. "Now I feel like I know her and I'd like to go see her."

> ❧ ❧ ❧
>
> "We recently held a 60th-year wedding anniversary for my grandparents. It was the reunion we always dreamed of—the most joyous, love-filled celebration ever! I met cousins and relatives that I'd never before met, but felt I knew well... all because of our family newsletter."
>
> **— Lisa**

From Eyes to Heart to Hands

It's All Relative is one of many types and lengths of newsletters to choose from. The purpose of this book is to take the family newsletter idea, let the examples and text enter in through your eyes, settle into your heart and then come back through the creations from your hands.

Flip quickly through the pages of this book and you'll see many newsletter formats and styles—letters, poems, photo scrapbooks, cards, genealogy, e-mail and Web sites. Preschool children can send their messages through

their drawings and artwork. Photo bugs can capture the moments with pictures. Writers and poets can share through words. The examples celebrate all types of occasions including holidays, weddings, vacations, births and more. They show how to get your whole family involved and maybe even inspire your young ones into further interest in writing and publishing.

Realistically, we've all received boring letters and downer news. In the next chapter, you'll see how to create a message that assures news to bring "mailbox cheer." Then, you'll move into many different ideas for newsletters. On the pages throughout the book, you'll see yellow boxes with stories from people who have either written or received family news and the impact it makes on their spirits. In the back of the book are ready-to-use templates, worksheets for collecting stories and other information along with hundreds of ideas for what to write about, how to save money and more.

Keeping the Links Strong

If you ever feel like you're the only one who wants to keep your family close by, take a good look in airports, parking lots and lobbies everywhere (especially during the holiday season). You'll see tearful goodbyes, lingering bear hugs and the words, "I love you, Dad" coming out of the mouth of the most stoic corporate executive.

Okay, I'm an airport crier. Seeing families in airports reminds me of my own geographically distanced family. This book is for all of you who want to visit with your family and friends more often and want to send more than just a card with your signature. It's a celebration of family connections, filled with ideas and inspiration to make creating newsletters easy and fun.

Perhaps by keeping in regular touch through your own family news, those airport goodbyes will be easier. Join me in the rest of these pages and see ideas for creating your own newsletter get-together.

> ❦ ❦ ❦
>
> "Mom, when I start loving you, my mind has hearts all around it."
>
> — **Alyssa**, age 4, to her mother, in the Kid's Korner of *It's All Relative*

Our Latest Visitors

By Jay Fuentes, who was expecting a typical issue of IAR

It was again a pleasure receiving and reading *It's All Relative*. It gets better and more interesting every time.

Today for a change Rita seems to be a little better. Alexia made her so happy—you have no idea. Having her grandson, John, and his daughter was a double treat. What a joy family can be! Children today are like flowers in a garden. You can tell which ones have been fertilized with love. Let us never run out of this fertilizer.

We were very happy to hear Lisa and Terry had a pleasant few days visiting Vicki and Jason. Too bad you couldn't stretch it a little further to Deltona. Well maybe next time.

Alexia and Johnny brave the beach!

One reason we don't enjoy flying is the experience Johnny had in the Orlando airport. Imagine 4½ hours on a sit-still jet. I would have squeezed out through a porthole. Oops, Rita just corrected me; the time was spent at the airport, not the jet. I would have taken off like I was jet-propelled. And in conclusion, we love you all.

Johnny, thanks a million for bringing Alexia, she is a bubbly and intelligent child. You can't help but loving her. We loved how she took to the cold water. BRRRAVE!

We love you all.
Love, Nana & Pops

Through My Daughter's Eyes

By John Suarez

The earliest memories I have of Nana and Pop-Pop start when I was about five years old. I remember always being excited to see them, and Mom buying us new clothes to wear whenever we visited. I remember how fun it was when they came to see us in Puerto Rico. I remember always feeling loved, always special in their presence.

What I don't remember is how they actually treated me to make me feel that way. So when I took my five-year old daughter Alexia to meet her great-grandparents last month, I was

(Continued on page 6)

The article above was written in the "tribute" issue of *It's All Relative.* Many family members wrote in their memories and thoughts about their grandparents, Nana and Pops.

Every issue of the newsletter also includes an article from Pops (shown left). Read each of these articles and you'll see the basis for the strong family ties celebrated in the newsletter.

❦ ❦ ❦

"An old man's grandchildren are his glory..."

—Proverbs 17:6

Through My Daughter's Eyes
(Continued from page 1)

actually going back to my own childhood, to my earliest memories of Nana and Pop-Pop. And I relived the whole experience of being special through not only my own eyes, but my daughter's eyes as well.

One day Alexia came in the house and brought Nana a flower bud that had fallen to the ground in the backyard. Nana took the bud as if it were the most precious gift in the world and placed it in a water-filled vase on the counter. "Look what Alexia gave me," she said to Pop-Pop. "That sure is beautiful," he said, and Alexia just smiled with pride. I suspect that five-year old girl felt good every time she walked past the little bud vase. I know I did.

Pop-Pop went with Alexia and me one day to a playground at a nearby park. He hobbled through the sand with pain in his back, love in his heart and a camera in his hand as his great-granddaughter played with her daddy. It was all he could do to follow us around from the slide to the swings to the wooden monkey bars, but he helped preserve the Kodak moments so we could enjoy them again and again and again.

And so it went for five short days, from Daytona Beach to Disney World, after which I rediscovered what I must have felt some 30 years ago:

Nothing I did was unimportant to them!

Every ounce of their existence has been dedicated to helping the five-year old in all of us stay safe, happy, and young at heart. My daughter and I now have that in common. She cried almost all the way to the airport as we were leaving, and I knew exactly how she felt. Alexia loves her Nana and Pop-Pop, too.

And I realized how wonderful it was to know people whose purpose it has been to help us celebrate our own lives. It seems only fitting to take a little time to celebrate theirs. We are all better people because of them. Is there a greater gift than that?

Nana and Pop-Pop, I love you both. Thank you for being great grandparents to me, and great Great-grandparents to my daughter. Thank you for making a difference.

Love, Johnny and Alexia

Do I Dare?

If you read the Ann Landers and Dear Abby columns, you may be asking yourself if you dare do a newsletter. You're not alone. This Ann Landers column reflects how many families have stopped doing newsletters in fear that theirs was one of the "boring" ones.

Reprint permission granted by Ann Landers and Creators Syndicate.

Boring Or Not, Holiday Newsletters Are Wanted

Dear Ann Landers: When we moved to Canada from the States 10 years ago, we knew it would be difficult to keep up with all our friends, but we were certain we'd hear from everyone at Christmas. Those wonderful newsletters and pictures of their kids were a great way to stay in touch.

Now, thanks to your column about what a bore annual newsletters are, we didn't receive even one this past season. The year before, we received 10.

Obviously, our friends read your column and take it seriously. They didn't want to come off as bores or braggarts, so they didn't tell us how their daughter's graduation went, if they had fun on their trip to the Orient or anything personal. With all the employment problems these days, we'd like to be assured that our friends are still working.

A signature on a holiday greeting card doesn't tell us much, although we did get some lovely cards from our insurance agent, our dentist, our financial consultant and a number of business associates. We really miss those great newsletters from our friends.

Thanks, Ann, for making last Christmas a little less cheery and a lot more remote. You really did a number on St. Nick.

BAH, HUMBUG!
IN EDMONTON

I apologize for discouraging folks from sending those newsy chronicles loaded with personal details. Please reactivate the tradition. Obviously, I'm out of the loop. □

Here it is March, and I'm still getting blistering letters for putting the kibosh on Christmas newsletters. Yours was one of several. So — let it be known to one and all that I take it back. Start now to gather facts for your 1996 Christmas newsletter.

Don't leave out anything. People really do want details of your face lift and tummy tuck, your daughter-in-law's tubal ligation and your husband's hair transplant. Tell them about your cocker spaniel's litter, and if you have a photo of your daughter in her ballet costume, send it along with a copy of the letter from your alderman thanking you for helping him get re-elected.

Chapter One:
Think Before You Ink

When did family newsletters get such a bad reputation? I'd often wondered until I started putting together this book. You see, I've been asking everyone I know the same question: "Have you received any good family newsletters lately?" The answer has been surprisingly consistent. "Oh, we've received some. But not any *good* ones."

The bad newsletters lead to other bad newsletters—since they're the only ones people can use as models when they sit down to create their own newsletter. It's time to change that. Let's tackle the problem spots right now and then move into showing examples of successful family newsletters.

This chapter guides you through some of the do's and don'ts. It helps you select the publication format best suited to the materials you have on hand and to your capabilities and interests.

Watch Out for These Trouble Spots

Problem: **Time of severe trauma or sadness**. The death of a loved one or other times of sadness make it hard (or sometimes impossible) to write or result in a very sad newsletter.

Solution: Many newsletter creators miss an issue from time to time because "they just can't" put together the newsletter. Others get contributions from others (see page 90) to pull the family together through the difficult times. Others wait until later and then make a short statement telling what has happened and thanking family and friends for their support.

Problem: **Right amount of detail**. Short newsletters that read like laundry lists or long newsletters telling readers more than they ever wanted to know.

Solution: If you're having trouble filling the newsletter, see pages 77 to 87 for content ideas. If you have trouble shortening the news, ask a friend to help you. Ask a few people to read your newsletter and highlight the most interesting information (see worksheet on page 88). Save the long version for your scrapbook and shorten down the final letter.

> "We were going to discontinue our family newsletter because we kept seeing letters in Ann Landers column about how people hate these cheery Christmas letters... but we got so many cards saying, 'We missed your annual update!' so we decided to roll it out again this year. *Mahalo* from Hawaii to all of your readers."
>
> **—Sam Horn**

Problem: **Health updates**. Describing unpleasant details such as deaths, surgery or pain in timeline or detailed fashion.

Solution: Make one statement telling what has happened after waiting for the event to take perspective. Devote the detail of unpleasant events to describing how you are thankful for the help that family or friends gave you during the trying time (see yellow box to the left). If a loved one has passed, consider sharing memories of a special time.

❧ ❧ ❧

Problem: **Children's accomplishments**. Discussing children's grades, trophies, awards, teacher conferences, sports results.

Solution: Have the children write about themselves. Or, ask them questions and write using their words. Write about or show photos of children's specific gifts and talents such as their favorite school subjects. Mention what the children are doing, not quantifying how they are winning.

Here's an example of effective news of children:

"The children are doing great. Patrick and Keenan did really well in school the previous six weeks. Patrick received A's and B's in all his classes and Keenan earned S's. They both need to improve their reading skills, and Keenan is going to have to learn to concentrate for a full day of school. But, all in all, they are doing excellent.

"Sara is doing exceptionally well in 'Daddy's School.' She's an expert in the installation of sprinkler systems, laying sod and installing basketball goals. In the next semester, we are planning an agricultural class, a fence installation class and techniques to escape trouble from behind trees and in the rough by utilizing a weak left hand grip to slice the ball."

❧ ❧ ❧

Problem: **Parent's accomplishments**. Telling so much about a business venture that it seems like a sales pitch.

Solution: If your friends are interested in your business, put them on your business mailing list. This way, they'll receive separate mailings that keep them up to date on your ventures.

For both parents and children, let everyone create their own brag list. List it as a "Brag List" and use a numbered or bulleted list.

❧ ❧ ❧

Problem: **Hard to read text**. People have trouble reading long lines of type, no matter how interesting or fun it is.

Solution: Increase the page margins to at least one inch on each side.

❧ ❧ ❧

Problem: **Bats and Balls!!!** (School-teachers' lingo for exclamation points.) Every other sentence ends with an exclamation point.

Solution: Let your writing and content share your enthusiasm. It's much more effective than !!!!'s. Save them for the punch line or surprise ending of a story or joke.

❧ ❧ ❧

❧ ❧ ❧

Good example of sharing health news:

"We did have a scare in April. John underwent emergency surgery for an aneurysm of the aorta. He came close to not making it, but after a long and successful recovery he is 100% again. We thank God for watching over him and give considerable credit for his recovery to the many, many prayers and well wishes that were sent his way."

—Elinor

Miscellaneous Notables

❑ Balance vacation and trip news with everyday news.

❑ When including news of kids, describe them for the people who've never met them. "Johnny is five and Susan is eight" doesn't tell much.

❑ Define relationships. For example, "Kate was the flower girl in Chris's (my nephew) wedding."

❑ With letters, consider sending a photo.

❑ Unless writing a newsletter solely for your children's scrapbooks, avoid referring to yourselves as "Mommy" and "Daddy."

❑ Watch for overuse of baby language—even when put in quotes.

❑ Watch for overuse of jargon and common expressions (if you find yourself wanting to put it in quotes—things like "Supermom," "Mommy's little helper," "set up shop," etc. look for another way to say it).

❑ Avoid using the mailmerge feature of word processing to personalize the salutation. Instead, handwrite a personal note.

❑ Avoid news of lawsuits.

❑ Explain who's in photos.

❑ Do not apologize for sending a newsletter in the opening paragraph. Consider using humor instead to acknowledge that not everyone likes newsletters. (See example below.)

See news questions and content ideas on pages 77 to 87 for more inspiration.

Kathie has fun with the back page of her newsletter warning recipients that it's a family newsletter.

Decision-Making Chart

Avoid most of the trouble spots by selecting a newsletter format that's suited to your interests. Consider a photo-only newsletter or a mindmap newsletter (see page 74). Or, your news may be part of a larger family Web site. Decisions, decisions. Here's a quick planning list to help you decide which type of newsletter you'd like to create.

Here are some common purposes for newsletters. *Check those that apply to you:*

❏ Share news of extended family.

❏ Share genealogical information.

❏ Update friends and family.

❏ Bring scattered family closer together.

❏ Promote attendance at annual family reunion.

❏ Celebrate special family holidays.

❏ Share news of births.

❏ Continue family traditions and crafts.

❏ Share advice.

❏ Keep in touch with new addresses.

❏ Mourn the passing of family members.

❏ Other:_____

Here are some common things that readers enjoy. *Check those that you can include:*

❏ Pictures of people

❏ Pictures of places

❏ Highlights

❏ Jokes

❏ Trivia

❏ Funny things that happened

❏ Happy things that happened

❏ Interesting things that the kids said

❏ Stories of everyday-life subjects (playing outside, hobbies, favorite books)

How often do you want to update or publish?

❏ Yearly *(publish an end of the year or holiday update)*

❏ Quarterly *(design a two-page seasonal update)*

❏ Monthly *(write a one-page letter-style newsletter)*

❏ Weekly *(use an e-mail newsletter)*

❏ Occasionally *(set up a personal or family Web page)*

What do you enjoy doing? *Check those that apply to you:*

❏ Writing *(see pages 32 to 41)*

❏ Poetry *(see pages 38, 39 and 72)*

❏ Photography *(see pages 10 to 21)*

❏ Drawing *(see pages 25 to 27)*

❏ Scrapbooking *(see pages 16 to 18, 21, 24, 63)*

❏ Working on the computer *(see pages 42 to 57)*

❏ Collecting genealogical information *(see pages 54 to 57)*

❏ Humor *(see pages 35, 37 and 62)*

❏ Reunion planning *(see page 53)*

❏ Learning about new technology like the Internet *(see pages 58 to 67)*

❏ Other:_____

How much time do you want to spend per issue?

❏ 1 hour *(try an e-mail newsletter or handwrite on a template)*

❏ 3 hours *(use a letter-style format)*

❏ 5 hours *(consider a traditional newsletter)*

❏ a day *(publish multiple pages)*

❏ longer than a day *(start on your family memoirs)*

To how many people do you want to send your news?

❏ Less than 10 *(send personal notes with news)*

❏ 11-50 *(make photo newsletters on a color copier or ink jet printer)*

❏ 51-100 *(use pre-printed papers)*

❏ Over 100 *(make black and white copies; self-mail; consider postcards)*

❏ Over 200 *(consider Web publishing or e-mail news)*

What is your budget? *(For a mailing list of 50 people)*

❏ $0 *(use e-mail)*

❏ $1 to $15 *(design a postcard)*

❏ $15 to $25 *(write a letter-style newsletter, copy in black)*

❏ $25 to $50 *(find pre-printed stationery, print in color)*

❏ $50 to $100 *(design a four-page newsletter; mail in envelopes)*

❏ Over $100 *(go wild!)*

Also see "Ways to Stretch Your Budget" in the NewsTools section on page 103.

❧ ❧ ❧

"I enjoy being the collection point for the family information. This way a family member only needs to write one letter and all the rest of the family will receive it in the newsletter."

— **Jerry**

❧ ❧ ❧

"Newsletters that go to widely scattered readers who rarely see one another are crucial to the reader's perception of the group. They set the tone for other members. In fact, such newsletters quite often are to readers the association they represent—something they can hold in their hands, share with others. Thoughtful planning of these publications is especially important. Be sure they project the image that you want to project."

—**Helen Ashmore**
The Newsletter Editor's Handbook

Start a series.
Creating a series turns your photos into news by showing growth and change over time. Have studio pictures taken once or twice a year. Lisa does this at Christmastime and Easter every year for her four girls. Look closely and see the girls grow up frame by frame.

10 Brooke
Blair 10

Blair 9
Brooke 9

Berkeley 8

Blair 8
Bridgette 8

Berkeley 6

Blair 6yrs
Bridgette 6

Blair 3
Brooke 3yrs

Chapter Two:
You Ought to Be in Pictures

Do you enjoy taking photographs? Do you have a shoebox-full sitting around? Are you too busy to write, or do you feel like the "writing gene" was taken by other family members?

This chapter shows how to bring mailbox cheer with great photos. It includes tips for taking, selecting and readying photos for publication. If you have a camera or access to photos, a photo development service, a few crafts supplies and a photocopying service, you have everything it takes to publish a photo or scrapbook newsletter.

Photos in newsletters make the greeting more human, fun and warm. Our eyes are naturally attracted to photos—especially those of people. That said, make sure your photos send the desired message. You may be writing "a great time was had by all" in the newsletter, but if the kids look bored in the photo, your readers will believe the photo.

Babies and puppies. Years ago, advertisers found that the best way to attract people to a page is with photos of babies or puppies. Get a baby with the puppy and you've got 'em hooked!

🍎 🍎 🍎

"We can all be inspired to make our lives within our families full of fun and meaning and an essential kind of energy. And it can happen not only on special days like holidays but also on regular days, those marching Mondays and Tuesdays and Wednesdays that make up the bulk of our time spent here on this planet. Life is for nothing if not for celebrating."

—Elizabeth Berg, writing in *Family Traditions*

❦ ❦ ❦

"A family's photo-
graph album is gen-
erally about the
extended family—
and, often, is all that
remains of it."

—Susan Sontag
U.S. essayist,
On Photography

Tips for the Staging

The best newsletter photos are those that mix candid shots with posed ones. Many family newsletters emphasize the vacations and holidays. My guess is that those events are remembered more because the camera is handy. What about everyday life? Is the camera, or the presence of the camera, skewing our memories for the year? Keep your camera loaded and at hand for the everyday moments.

When an event is going on, look for the "warm and fuzzy" quotient—the smiles, hugs, hand-holding, people close together. Everyone understands this body language. In her book, *Family Traditions* (see Publishing Tools on page 104), author Elizabeth Berg tells of the observations of her friend, a flight attendant. He can tell the families who've had a good vacation together. "Some families are all smiles, so relaxed… they sort of lean into each other all the way home."

These "lean" pictures are the ones that will communicate a good time on vacation much more than the stand-in-front-of-the-monument shot.

Tips for the Taking

Luckily, family newsletters have leeway that professional publications do not—it's okay and even preferable to look "folksy." That said, once you have camera in hand, a few tips can make everyone happier with their photo (i.e. your teenager won't fuss about the photo you want to show).

Every family has an infamously bad photographer. Maybe she's known for cutting the heads off the taller members of the group shot. Or, perhaps he's notorious for the long setup, forcing everyone to hold fake smiles for intolerable periods of time. Our family has a Cameo Bandit, who ambushes people who have mouths full of food and unattractive facial expressions.

Photos are an essential part of preserving family history. But too many family photos inspire comments like "It's good of everyone but Uncle Fred" or "If only Joe's eyes weren't closed." In his book, *The World's Best & Easiest Photography Book* (see page 105), photo expert Jerry Hughes says that anyone can take good photos with a simple camera by following these tips.

1. For indoor shots, make sure your subjects are standing at least three feet from the background. If they're too close to a wall, the flash will create a shadow behind them, especially if the room is not strongly lit.

2. Take outdoor shots early in the morning or late in the afternoon, ideally with the sun behind the subjects. In the middle of the day, the sun is at its harshest and causes subjects to squint.

3. Use a zoom or telephoto lens to compress the frame and soften the background. Avoid wide angle lenses, which expand the frame and add pounds to subjects.

4. Try to show people in action rather than at rest. Even posed shots can be active, with family members talking in a group or gathered around a piano.

5. Have your subjects turn slightly sideways to the camera, for both individual and group shots. Posing at an angle, with most of the weight on one leg, is more flattering and thinning.

Before and afters.
Consider showing before and after pictures to celebrate:
• anniversaries
• home remodeling
• weight loss
• birthdays
• graduations
• vacations

Selecting the Best Photos to Use

So, you have your stack of photos from your vacation or from the reunion. How do you select the best ones? Here are some tips.

1. **Be true to the event**. Select the shots that best represent the overall feeling of the day. Look for the photos that lend reality and emotion to the page.

2. **Look for action**. Balance dynamic with static photos. A group shot is static. Static photos represent solidity, tradition and family foundation. Dynamic pictures show action and represent the future, the movement and energy of the family.

3. **Look for angle**. Look for unusual angles to represent a fresh viewpoint. For agile photographers, they may mean climbing to a high spot or lying down to show a more dramatic angle.

4. **Look for comparison/contrast**. In group shots, the relative importance of group members can be expressed in unusual or striking arrangements with one person front and center and other members in the background. This may have the family matriarch and/or patriarch in the lead "duck" positions with the rest of the family fanning out into a V.

5. **Look for character.** For individual portraits, take both formal and candid poses, searching for unique qualities in the character of the subject. Catch the moment when an attitude is struck.

6. **Watch for the unusable**. Avoid using pictures that essentially show nothing—that are too fuzzy or taken from too far away.

A "disposable" idea. Send everyone in your family a disposable camera along with instructions:

- No more than three posed shots.
- At least one candid shot of each family member doing something that they love to do.

(Above, from *It's All Relative*) Note how closeness can be communicated by wrapped arms and holding hands.

(Left) Unless sleeping, few toddlers are ever at rest. This dynamic duo are caught in play action. (This photo is used in the newsletter shown on page 21.)

Size photographs so that people's faces are at least as large as a thumbprint. Otherwise, it's hard to recognize who's in the picture.

Tell the story in two frames. If you want to show a building, house or scene along with people, consider using two pictures. See page 45. Note how Polly and Bob's new house is shown in one photo and Polly and Bob in the other. If they tried to show both in the same frame, Polly and Bob would be too small.

Readying Pictures for the Page

Once pictures have been developed or scanned into your computer, they can often be improved before placing them on the page. This is done through cropping, sizing and editing.

Cropping. You can make most pictures better by cropping—trimming off irrelevant elements or blank spaces. Look for the main point of the picture and decide what can be cut off to emphasize it. Vary sizes and shapes of photos used on your page. Try long, narrow pictures.

Sizing. In most newsletters, photos are too small. Vary the sizes of pictures on one page. Find the most interesting one and run it larger than the others. Strive for variety and emphasis. That said, if you increase the size of a photo too much, it may get grainy. For crisp reprints on the page, it is usually better to reduce than to enlarge photographs.

Photo editing. Computer programs allow you to "fix" problems in photos. These include capturing that trademark, dimpled grin on Aunt Carmen's face only to get the film back and find that the tree that was behind her looks like it's growing out of her head. Using either a computer program or a good pair of scissors or artist's knife and a steady hand, you can create a silhouette instead.

Give your photos more zest by showing their lifelike shape. To do this, clip out the background (called making a silhouette) either using scissors or a photo editing program on your computer.

Kid Quo

Roseanne Barr had the righ
She said, "I figure if the kids a
at the end of the day, I've do
job." We must have been doing a pretty go
because both boys are full of vim and vigor
beginning, middle, and close of the day. This

Form-fitting shapes. Use scissors or a computer to trim around the subject in a way that creates a dynamic shape.

Wishing you good hair days. Consider showing a closeup of one of the people in a photograph instead of the entire frame.

Top: The Bonney family reunion photographed by Bob Pattison.
Above: The Vizenor family reunion (see page 16 for the Vizenor family newsletter).

Special Needs of Group Photos

Photographing large groups is a challenge if you don't do this every day. Here are some tips from the "been there, done that."

❑ Hire a photographer.

❑ Set up the location before corralling the people.

❑ Organize singers to entertain the group while lighting is being set.

❑ Bring the children over at the last minute.

❑ For a "unified" look, photograph everyone in their reunion T-shirts or ask that everyone wear a certain color (see the Vizenor family above in blue).

🐛🐛🐛

"The last time Bob photographed the reunion group, he and his crew had just set up everything for an outside group picture… just as it started to rain. Now he's our official videographer!"

—Polly

❦ ❦ ❦

"My newsletter is a 'retirement hobby' intended to keep me busy and in close touch with my ever growing family ... and sharing my pride with others. (I'm 66, my bride is 63, we have 9 children, 18 grandkids, and recently our first great-grandchild.)"

—Charles

Proud Patriarch Learns Publishing as a Retirement Hobby

Charles (aka "Grampa") began writing the newsletter over five years ago at the request of his son who was moving out of state. His newsletter has kept its personal touch because of his manual "cut and paste" style and lively photo captions. Charles credits the newsletter for inspiring him to learn to type ("albeit still hunt and peck") and to learn to use a computer for word processing. He sends the publication monthly to over 100 people including someone in Wales.

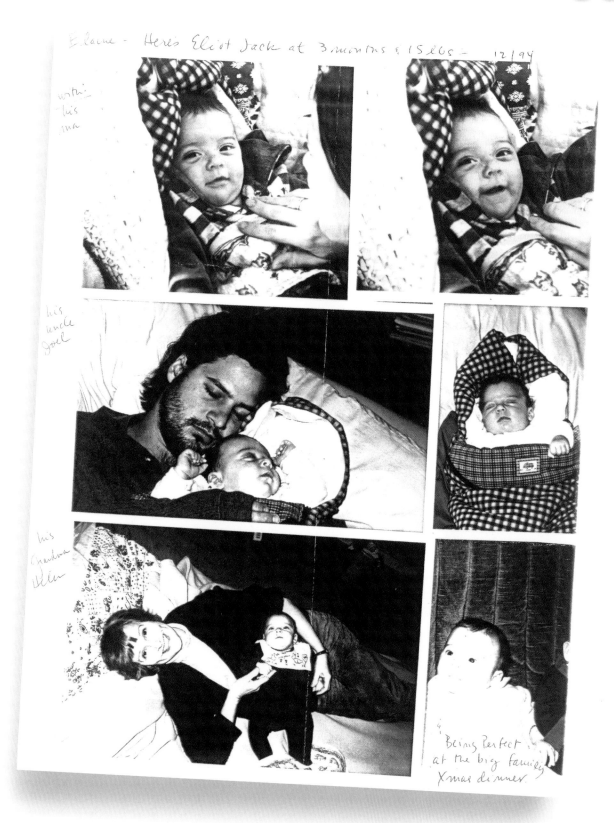

New Grandbaby Inspires Spontaneous Scrapbooking

Bohemian Grandma Helen put together this quick and easy scrapbook page after getting back a roll of photos from her first visit with her new grandbaby. The handwritten captions not only make the page easy to prepare, they also tie in well to the warm, soft emotions created by the pictures.

Your photo newsletter could have various themes such as "What was your favorite moment last year?" or, "What accomplishment are you most proud of for 1999?"

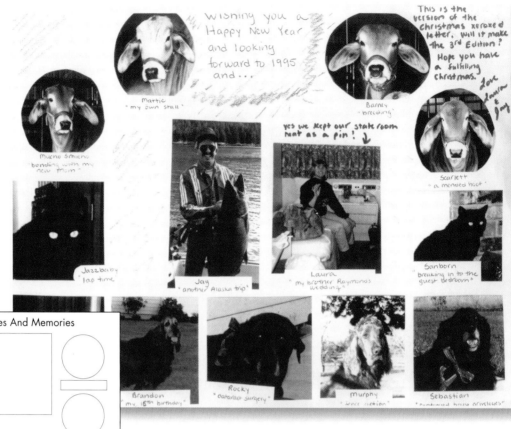

Welcome to the barnyard! This is a great example of a "no-tech" and little-writing newsletter. Photos were selected and trimmed and hand-written captions tell the story. Color photocopies were made from the master, by the "master."

🐾🐾🐾

"My husband and I don't have children — our 'babies' have fur. Sharing our pets with our friends turned out to be a real hit. I was really glad to have put this together because the next year we lost many of our elderly pets. This one sheet really captured each of their personalities."

— **Laura**

Paste on Pictures, Pen a Caption and Print!

Using the copy-ready template (shown above and provided in full size on page 111), you can create your own photo scrapbook for the year to send to family and friends. For best results, follow these tips.

❑ Choose a photo with a subject that fills each circle.

❑ Select a family or group photo for the middle rectangle (it's sized to hold a standard size print without having to trim).

❑ Handwrite or type in captions.

❑ When writing captions, identify the people or images shown. Tell the story behind the photo. Add significant or interesting facts that can't be gleaned from the picture (see worksheet on page 91).

When your master copy is ready, shop around for the best price on color photocopies. When at the copy shop, ask to see a sample copy first and request that color levels be adjusted (watch for skin tones that appear too yellow or red). A good copier operator can get the colors just right. If printing in black and white, set the copier on "halftone" or "photo" mode for best results. If printing on colored paper, avoid colors such as yellows and greens that are unflattering to skin tones.

Getting photos on the page:

- Scan them with your home scanner.
- Take them to a friend who has a scanner.
- Take them to a copy shop.
- Use photo screens (see Publishing Tools on page 108).
- Paste them directly on the original and copy.
- Have photos developed onto a CD-ROM.
- Use a digital camera.

❦ ❦ ❦

"My daughter was so proud of the picture she drew for this holiday portrait and postcard. We took several pictures and she was beaming in each one."

— **Nancy**

Getting Children Involved in Photographs

It's only too soon before a child's idea of "participation" is making bunny ears and devil horns behind an unsuspecting subject. Here are some ideas for getting kids involved in a way that everyone will enjoy.

❑ Involve children in deciding the theme for the photo.

❑ Let children select the clothing theme for the picture.

❑ Have each child draw a poster with a message for the photo.

❑ Let kids take some pictures.

❑ Let the kids select their favorite photos to use.

❑ Have kids choose a funny word to say instead of "cheese."

❑ Give kids extra copies of the photos to put in their rooms.

❑ Let kids decide the organization of a group shot (i.e. by height, gender, age, family, etc.).

❑ For the last frame or picture, give the kids free reign to do what they'd like. You may be pleasantly surprised with the results.

Sam Says . . .

This past year turned out even better than I could have imagined. I've enclosed a newsletter to bring you up to date about some of the good news concerning ACTION SEMINARS.

Tongue Fu! received a healthy advance from St. Martin's Press and will be their lead non-fiction book when it's officially released Jan. 22. In addition to a 12 city publicity tour, it will be featured in Cosmopolitan, Family Circle, and Essence magazines, and has received endorsements from many best-selling authors.

I received a FAX from a senior editor at Readers Digest saying how much she liked my style, and would I like to be a writer for them. Would I?! Who could have guessed when I was a young girl reading stacks of Reader's Digests at family gatherings (where kids were to be seen and not heard) that I would be blessed with this satisfying full-circle experience of being asked to be part of their staff?

St. Martin's Press has already requested another book, (Complete Confidence), and a specialized Tongue Fu! series (At Work, At School, etc.), so after the initial media blitz in February, I will settle back home and continue to write. That's fine with me because I love sitting at the computer and letting those creative juices flow . . . and it gives me a chance to be around to enjoy the kids' all-too-brief growing up years.

In addition to being President of the Hawaii chapter of the National Speakers Association, I helped organize and emcee the Maui Writers Conference at the Five Diamond Grand Wailea Resort. This event once again exceeded our expectations and the presenters (Eric Roth, screenwriter for Forrest Gump, Jack Canfield of "Chicken Soup for the Soul" fame, Barbara deAngelis, and John Saul) combined with over 700 participants to make for a magical four days.

My favorite '95 memory was Mother's Day. We rose at dawn to board the Trilogy catamaran and headed out for a day of exploring. We anchored off Makena Beach, donned our snorkel gear, dove into the clean water (100 foot visibility), joined hands and paddled around on the surface following the sea turtles as they glided through coral formations below us. Topside we enjoyed a bar-b-qued chicken lunch under the blue skies, and had the wind at our backs as we raced back to the harbor with the boys frolicking like lion cubs on the trampoline bow. Pure fun.

Kid Quo Pro

Roseanne Barr had the right idea. She said, "I figure if the kids are alive at the end of the day, I've done my job." We must have been doing a pretty good job, because both boys are full of vim and vigor at the beginning, middle, and close of the day. This is the only picture you'll *ever* see of them sitting down.

We subscribe to the philosophy that we'll drive them anywhere they'll sweat, so their weeks are filled with soccer, baseball, and basketball. Their nights are filled with our favorite activity . . . "walk and rolls." Andrew straps on his roller blades, Tom jumps on his bike, and I hoof it. We take off around the 'hood for an evening on our quiet community streets. We check out the stars, play with Furrball (our cat buddy who always comes to meet us), pluck some plumerias for our pillows, and kidnap (frognap?) any stray buffo's who are foolish enough to stray onto the street.

'Da boys joined the Symphony choir this year and treated us to an at-the-top-of-their-lungs preview performance of the Hallelujah chorus from the shower. Andrew is in 4th grade and Tom is in 6th ab junior high, (ARRGGHH! How did that happen?!) Both made student of the month for their classes.

Weekends we head down to our local user-friendly beach to take advantage of the best part of living in the islands, year round ocean play. The kids continue to make a good case for perpetual motion; they charge into the surf on their boogie boards and ride them in until they scrape their bellies on the beach. Out they go again, over and over, only stopping to play ball, delighting in making full-out diving catches into the surf. If we're lucky, the whales put in an appearance (between Dec. - April) and we marvel as they leap from the sea, breaching and flapping their flukes, presenting a spectacular backdrop to Tom and Andrew's energetic antics.

Hanging Out with the Horns in Hawaii

Doing newsletters comes naturally to writer and speaker Sam Horn, who uses one to promote her business, Action Seminars. Sam uses this newsletter to showcase photos and news of her family including these fun pictures of the beginning and end of a day on the ocean. (Sam is also the executive director of the Maui Writers Conference —now that's a good reason to go to Hawaii… all in the name of improving your family newsletter!)

❦ ❦ ❦

"I was happy to capture these two photos showing the boys at motion and at rest. It's pretty rare to catch our two perpetual motion machines sitting down. Seeing these photos brings back some great memories of that trip and this year."

— **Sam**

Alexandre and Daniele over-power the Belorussian kayak team.

Elaine and sister-in-law Kerana see the US women's soccer team win a gold. (This crowd was **not** what Bob Dole had in mind when he spoke of "Soccer Moms.")

Alexandre's 4th birthday high-light—Donna arrives from New Orleans with cake decorating sup-plies in hand to make a **blue backhoe** cake.

Two years old and chocolate!

VIP treatment by neighbor and Fire Dispatch Barb Pikesley.

Grandma's nature girl at the Oregon coast.

I ♥ trains!

Home, home on the range.

Pop in for some Christmas Cheer...

It's the Holiday Scrap Book!

> "I had so many cute pictures that could show the energy and personalities of the kids and I knew words couldn't do them justice. The photos were really dynamic, because Alex and Daniele were still young enough to come alive when the camera came out."
>
> **— Elaine**

Share Your Scrapbook in News Style

If you've already selected and grouped photos for your personal scrapbook, you can convert them to a scrapbook-style newsletter in minutes. Position photos on a letter-sized page, add captions to the photos following the tips on page 111 and photocopy onto colorful paper.

Newsletter

Chapter Three:
Handmade News

There's something very relaxing about creating with paper, scissors, glue and markers. It's something that a computer can't do for you. Even if you use the computer to produce the text and photos, you can get the whole group involved by adding other decorative elements. This chapter shows how to use different papers and folds, templates, stickers, stamps and markers to create colorful, charming newsletters.

You can use these techniques to make a one-of-a-kind news card for a friend or, with the lowering costs of photocopies, mass produce your masterpiece in color. Some people use colored paper to add zest to the newsletter but reproduce the text or drawings in black.

Tips for Selecting Papers

An important element in the newsletter's design is the paper you select. Look for papers that match the "feel" you're trying to communicate. For friendship letters, select your favorite color or a design that reminds your friends of you. Perhaps you're known for loving cats, fishing or tea pots. For school letters, find bright colored paper or your school colors. Birth announcement news is often scooped by the color of the paper—pink or blue. Wedding and anniversary news can be printed on pearled paper or the wedding colors. Many preprinted newsletter stationery designs are available for holiday newsletters.

If you're creating a news postcard, make sure the paper is heavy enough to travel safely through the postal system. Or, create a foldover card to give the piece extra bulk and seal it with a colorful sticker.

One last note on paper: watch out for paper colors that are too dark or backgrounds that are too busy. Ideally, you want your text and images to be as dark as possible and the background to be as light as possible. This contrast makes for the easiest read.

Handwritten in a Flash

If you're among the time-deprived around the holiday season, give this easy format a try. The template for the tree (shown above) is provided in the resources section on page 109. Enlarge on a photocopier and, using a black ink pen, fill in each circle using the following tips as a guide.

❑ Give each family member a circle to fill in.

❑ Reserve a circle for a message to friends and family.

❑ Alternatively, you could use the circles for family photos and write a letter-style newsletter on the back of the page.

❑ Have each family member sign a present. (Remember the pets, too!) If you need additional presents for the design, photocopy the template and cut and paste the presents.

When your master copy is ready, photocopy onto colored paper. You can find great colors at office supply stores and photocopy services. For more unique papers, shop your local art supply and stationary stores and catalogs (see Publishing Tools on page 108 for listings). To mail, fold and 1) insert in a holiday card, 2) put in an envelope on its own or with a photo, or 3) use stickers to hold shut and mail on its own.

❧ ❧ ❧

"I'm in the retail business so the holiday time is always very busy. This format allowed me to handwrite my news and have a fun newsletter out to family and friends in just a few minutes."

— **Kevin**

Take a trip to your local art supply store and browse the aisles for more decorative tools.

Decorating Pages for Extra Appeal

Whether you write your news by hand or with a computer, you can give a newsletter page extra excitement and dimension with stickers, glitter, ribbons or other fun decorations.

❏ Use ribbon or string to close the newsletter.

❏ Glue on buttons, sticks, pieces of fabric or leaves.

❏ Use rubber stamps to add a message to the envelope.

❏ Use stamp markers to decorate the margins of the pages.

❏ Punch out shapes on the corners of the pages. Use the punched pieces for confetti for the inside.

❏ Glue glitter to the cover for extra sparkle.

❏ Fold the paper in an unusual way (see pages 30 and 31).

Your kids are probably better with a mouse than you are. Many home computers come with a paint program that lets you draw pictures on the screen. Your child can create colorful drawings on the computer that you can print or import into a document. See programs for kids in Publishing Tools on page 107.

Illustrating News with Children's Artwork

Why use clip art if you have your own artists close at hand? Try any of these tips for getting your kids involved:

❏ Let children help with planning, even if it means letting them draw things you don't intend to use in your newsletter.

❏ Guide them on color choices; for instance, yellow doesn't always show up well if printing in black and white.

❏ Offer plenty of praise.

❏ If they're struggling with a particular shape, help them, but make sure you don't take over the drawing.

❏ Sometimes it's better to trust their judgment than to argue.

❏ You may not like the way the drawing is developing but wait until they're finished; you may be surprised with the results.

❏ Most importantly, it doesn't have to be perfect; kids color outside the lines—that's part of why Grandma thinks their pictures are so cute.

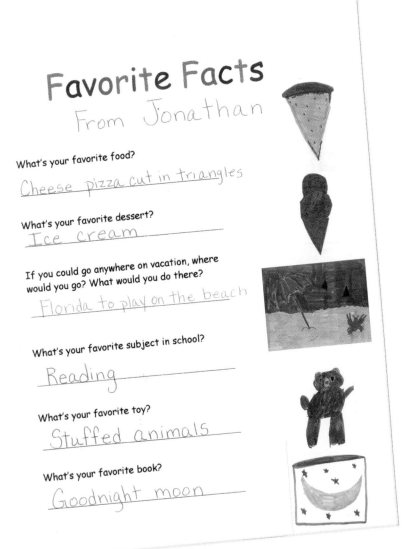

Favorite Facts
From Jonathan

What's your favorite food?
Cheese pizza cut in triangles

What's your favorite dessert?
Ice cream

If you could go anywhere on vacation, where would you go? What would you do there?
Florida to play on the beach

What's your favorite subject in school?
Reading

What's your favorite toy?
Stuffed animals

What's your favorite book?
Goodnight moon

❧ ❧ ❧

"My sister and her family live five states away. Knowing more about my niece and nephew— their favorite sports, food and movies— gives me something to talk with them about when they answer the phone. Otherwise, I end up asking what I call 'stupid aunt questions' or just asking to speak to my sister. Now, we have a chance to really catch up and get to know each other."

—Jennifer

Kids Share News in Their Own Words

If your children are too young to write, they can still share their news in their own words. Ask an older family member to interview young children. (See questions and form on pages 87 and 89). When interviewing:

❑ Tell kids why you're asking the questions.

❑ If you're getting one-word answers, make the questions less formal; start a conversation about their favorite things.

❑ Offer reminders if they're stuck for a particular answer, but the answers should be theirs, not yours.

❑ Ask them what other things the letter's recipient (i.e., Grandma) should know about them.

❑ Let your child interview you with the same questions.

❑ With two or more kids, let them interview each other.

❑ Encourage journal keeping and have them look through old journals for interesting stories.

❑ Tape record their answers and save the tape, so that years later, you'll have a recording of their voices from when they were young.

School News
by Jonathan

First grade is fun. At first it was hard to be in school all day, but my teacher is nice. Her name is Mrs. Allen and she has brown hair and glasses.

My favorite subjects are reading and science. We did a cool science experiment with celery and colored water. My best friend at school is David. We play

kickball and tag at recess.

I got my report card last week. I got four A's and one B (get those dollar bills ready, Grandpa). My conduct grade was pretty good, but I need to learn to keep my desk neater.

When I get home from school, I like to ride my bike and play with my friends. I also like to play with my dog.

te: Nov. 9th
e: 6
ade: 1st

A Fun and Informative Way to Share School Pictures

Try this format to send a "mantle-ready" card to relatives. Older kids can type or handwrite their own messages. While younger kids probably can't type, you can ask them questions and write the answers in paragraph form (see the questions on page 87 for ideas). Even if the message is typed, leave plenty of room for the child to sign the card.

If older kids need prompting to write a letter, offer suggestions or ask questions that help them find ideas. This pre-planning makes letter writing less of a chore.

Snow People Bring Out the Kid in All of Us

Involve the entire family in selecting photos and adding captions to a photo template such as this. For other template options, see the scrapbooking section of your local art supply store or a scrapbooking book at your bookstore. Use stickers for thought bubbles to add captions and comments.

❑ Let each family member select the photo they like of themselves.

❑ Ask each person to write or tell you the caption to use.

❑ If photocopied in black and white, use markers to colorize each newsletter.

❑ Create two versions: one generic for the majority of your list and one to be personalized for special family members such as grandparents.

❑ For a personalized newsletter, leave the captions blank and then add a message to each person.

❑ Save a copy or the original in your scrapbook.

Make your own winter scene by photocopying, cutting and arranging the "snow family," sled and winter scene provided in the back of the book after page 108.

Making Art from the Ordinary with Fun Folds

Starting with a standard letter-sized piece of paper you can create unusual shapes and sizes. Give some of these folds a try.

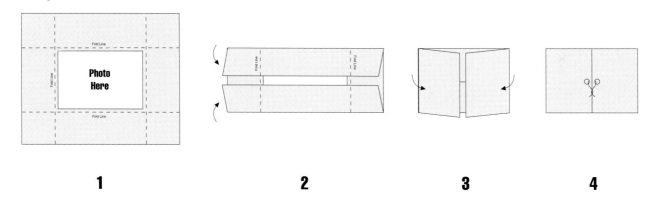

1   **2**   **3**   **4**

Open the door for the family photo. Place a standard-sized print in the middle of a page turned lengthwise. Fold top and bottom edges over and then turn side pieces in. Use tape, stickers, buttons or string to close the "door." Place in envelope or mail on its own.

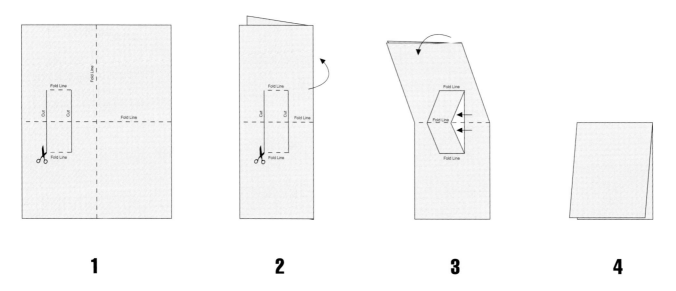

1   **2**   **3**   **4**

Make your own pop-up card. Copy, tape or paste a photo in the middle of the left size of the sheet (as shown in step 1). Using scissors or an artist's knife, cut along the right- and left-hand side of the photo. Fold the right side of the sheet back around the left side (shown in step 2) and glue shut. Take care not to glue the area with the photo. Pull photo area forward and fold (shown in steps 3 and 4).

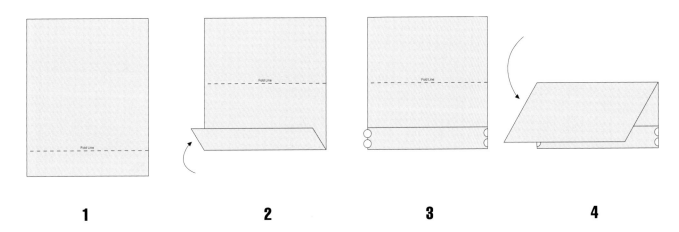

1 **2** **3** **4**

Send photos and other fun things in a pouch. Create a letter with a pouch by folding up a bottom section of the page and fastening it with tape, stickers or glue. Fold the resulting page (as shown in step 3) in half and mail in an envelope or on its own.

For more fun folds, see the book series, *How to Fold*, listed in Publishing Tools on page 105.

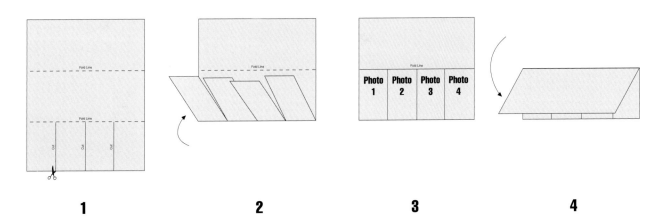

1 **2** **3** **4**

You'll flip over this. Make your own flip-down windows by cutting the bottom section of the page into four flaps. Fold up the flaps and then fold the top section over. Place photos on the outside or inside of the flaps. If the outside is a photo, place a message from the person (or people) in the photo on the area underneath or directly behind the flap.

From Our House to Yours...

Dear Friends and Family,

I know that I'm supposed to wait until the holidays to send you the annual newsletter but so much has been happening that you'll be hearing from us twice this year.

Moving never gets any easier
How quickly we forget what it was like to be the new kids on the block. Finding friends, soccer teams and social pals seems to get harder as the years go by. We think often of all of you —our friends we've met from city to city—and have faith we'll find good friends in St. Louis, too. (It's so stressful hiding our obnoxious sides until people start to like us!)

Hänsel was here
Our new little bungalow is in a formerly Swiss-German section of St. Louis and is filled with charming features like real woodwork and stained glass windows. The house was built in the late 40s but was completely renovated before we bought it. Alex and I joke that we're now "denovating" it with wall scratches from moving and unspeakable baby stains on the carpet.

Taking the parenthood plunge
Two days after summer solstice, our little bundle of drool arrived into the world. Alexandre, being the boy genius he is, realized what inept parents we are and decided to take it easy on us. Sleeping, eating, and teething have presented little problems to date, save family members who think we deserve much worse. (What? Weren't we angels?)

Mystery solved
I always wondered why parents send photographs of their children rather than photos of themselves of the entire family. It's simple. The children always look cute. The parents, poor neglected souls, need much more work.

So, no parent pictures with this letter but we wanted you all to know our new address. Please co and visit next time you're in the wonderful mid-West!

Elaine

Tips for Letter-Style Newsletters

The most common format for family newsletters is the letter style. These can be handwritten, typed on an old typewriter or produced using word processing software on a computer. To keep the format easy to read, follow these guidelines.

❏ Avoid paragraphs over five lines long.

❏ Give each paragraph a mini-headline. Use a bold font for it.

❏ Print on colorful paper.

Paper and envelope © Weedn Studios by The Paper Center, Inc. (available at Kinko's)

Chapter Four:
The News "Letter"

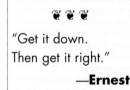

When you bring in the day's mail, what do you open first? Chances are that it's anything that's addressed by hand that has the look of a letter from a friend. The most effective letter-style newsletters are written in the same style as a personal letter.

If you have access to a typewriter or word processor and a photocopier, you have all the tools you need to create a family letter. The form letter is the most common type of family newsletter and is often included along with a card at the holiday times. This chapter gives you ideas for creating letters and writing the text for other newsletter types. We'll tackle the common concerns such as getting in the mood to write, what to write about and making a text-only newsletter attractive.

Warming Up to Write

The hardest part of writing is starting. The problem isn't lack of inspiration or motivation—it's perfectionism. We want what we write to be good, and we expect it to just come out that way. But, just as you wouldn't expect to be able to shop, cook and wash dishes at the same time, nor should you expect your words to magically appear.

Try writing in three steps. First, do a little prewriting and plan what you're going to write about. Then write your story based on the plan and the ideas you came up with in your prewriting. Finally, reread, revise and rewrite your story, filling in details and making any corrections.

Prewriting techniques include brainstorming, timelines, outlining and clustering.

Brainstorming is a way to get your family involved in generating story ideas. Have people call out ideas for people or events to write about. The group will feed off each other and will come up with suggestions they couldn't have thought of on their own.

Timelines allow you to remember and capture the events of the past year. Draw a line representing the year, add divisions for months, seasons or holidays, and write in the significant events that occurred in each. This helps you remember and gives a more accurate portrait of the entire year.

> ❦ ❦ ❦
> "Get it down. Then get it right."
> —**Ernest Hemingway**

> ❦ ❦ ❦
> "My mother did family letters most years as I was growing up. She recently photocopied them all for each of us kids as a record of our lives. What a gift!"
> —**Kathie**

For more help with your first draft, see Idea Tools and Writing Tools on pages 77 to 101.

Outlines don't have to be the formal diagrams you remember from Freshman English. Instead, use an outline to map the organization of a story. What kind of an introduction will you use? What information goes first? How should the story end? You can use brief descriptions to come up with a framework, and then fill in the details later.

Clustering or mapping helps you make associations and see connections. Write a word or short phrase (such as "reunion" used in the example below) in the middle of a page. Draw a circle around it. Write down the first thing that comes to mind when you think of the subject word. Draw a circle around that and draw a line connecting it to the first circle. Continue building from the original word or phrase by drawing a web or network with links and connections around it. Once you're finished, look at the outside circles for good stories. In the example below, that would be "secret recipe," "kids' messy faces," "mud puddle" and so on.

Your newsletter could be the cluster itself. (See Nancy's mindmap newsletter on page 74.)

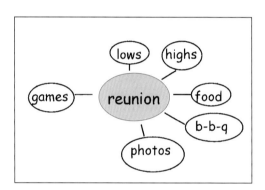

Clustering on the word *reunion* leads to main categories like food, games and photos (at left) and then to details about the volleyball game, the dog spilling the punch bowl, and the family farm (below). Notice how the details get more specific the farther the circles are from the hub; details like these would bring your reunion story to life.

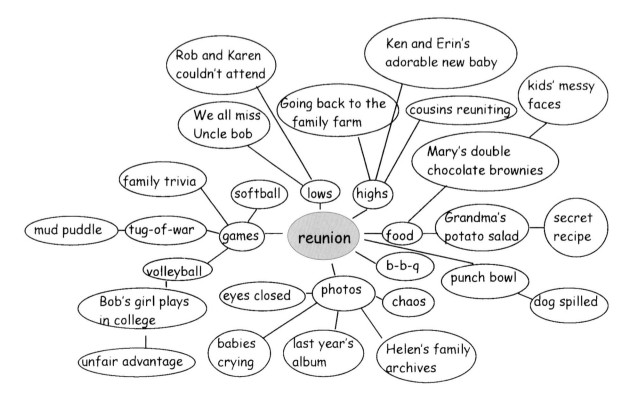

1997 Dillogram
Seasons Greetings y'all!

Another year has flown by and life is especially hectic this time of the year. Ya think we could start a movement to celebrate the holidays in May??? Here's one of those dreaded newsletters to fill you in on my life here in New Orleans this past year.

I didn't think I had travelled much this past year but looking back, I did pack my bags fairly often-mostly for work but sometimes with nice sidetrips. In May, I drove to Dallas for an Industrial Hygiene Conference (doesn't that sound exciting!) Actually, it's always nice to see former Texaco IH types at the schmoozefests plus I had a nice stay w/a former soccer teammate & her husband. In July, FEMA deployed me for 2 weeks in the funky, recently-flooded metropolis of Grand Forks, ND. It took my sinuses weeks to recover! A few days ago, FEMA asked me to go to Guam to work the typhoon relief operation but unfortunately my schedule was too tight. Bummer!

The drive to Dallas was a nice road test for my new Dillomobile-a used 4Runner. I'd wanted one of these vehicles since before they were known as SUVs! After driving a Celica low rider for so many years it sure is nice to slip in/out of my car with ease. Of course, my license plate is still RMDILLO.

This summer I officially hung up my soccer cleats and now enjoy the less painful sport of spectating (i.e. drinking & heckling) along the sidelines. I don't miss the aches, pains or early morning games but I do miss playing. I still work w/ the league in planning the Mardi Gras Ball tournament and often see many soccer pals at our local pro team's games. (formerly the "N.O. Gamblers"-now known as the less degenerate-sounding "Storm". I think the "N.O. Corruption" is a good name for a team...)

In September, I did safety & IH audits at Mattel facilities in Tijuana and Monterrey, MX. Barbie dolls and boogie boards! Very interesting stuff--life afta NAFTA! I managed to tag on a pre-audit visit with my Dad and Katy at their casa in Laguna Hill's "Laguna World." Also squeezed in a brief rendevous at the San Diego airport with my old Tucson pal Ilene. After the 2 business trips in Mexico, I immediately went back for a vacation trip to Isla Mujeres (off the coast of Cancun) with Ken and about 18 other New Orleanian turistas. The weather was kinda rainy (blame it on El Nino) but the beachfront hotel and margaritas from the cabana bar were straight out of a Jimmy Buffet songbook!

This has been a busy and profitable year of consulting. In addition to the usual stuff, I'm starting to do expert witness work (for the defense!) related to asbestos litigation. (groan!) I've also agreed to teach a Principles of IH course at Tulane next semester that will be videotelecast to a distance learning center in Richland, WA at the same time it's taught here in NO. At this point tho, I don't know WHY I agreed to do this--it ought to work out to about $5/hr! (double groan!!)

Weekly Scrabble games, monthly poker club, occasional sails on the Red Apple and annual N.O. events (Jazz Fest, Mardi Gras, etc.) seem to fill in the rest of the year. How do you people with kids manage? As usual, I'll be in Phoenix for the annual gathering of the clan at my mother's house. Here's wishing you and yours a happy, healthy, and safe holiday/New Year.

There's Nothing Generic Here

Sue really let her personality shine through in this letter-style newsletter. The fun graphic at the top highlights her hobby (collecting all things armadillo) and explains the newsletter's name. The writing style is conversational and entertaining while including plenty of news to catch readers up on Sue's past year. All of the graphic elements are clip art imported by a word processor.

Leave room on your newsletter page to add a personal note in the same ink color.

Merry Christmas

~ *and here's to the best New Year!*

A lot of changes have taken place in 1986. I'm no longer in uniform (much to Greg's dismay — not only does he miss the Captain's salary, but now I need civilian work clothes!) I did complete the Advance Course. Now I'm an Account Executive for Richmond Surroundings Magazine (a new city magazine). I sell advertising space. Straight commission sales are scary — and it is sometimes hard to stay motivated — but the potential is great — and it's a lot more fun than pharmaceutical sales! Besides, I've always wanted to work on a magazine.

Greg is doing great — he is on the Major's list — that means he'll make major sometime in '87 (hopefully, unless they really slow promotions down). He finished his 18 months of command of the 555 MP Co. on 3 October — and will be taking command of the CID (Criminal Investigation Division) Field Office here at Ft Lee during Dec. So we will be at Ft Lee for at least 2 more years. (Altho' we may have to move to other quarters when they renovate these.)

Greg got out to Oregon a few times this year — and was able to buy property on the coast — not on the water — but overlooking it. So now we need to do up plans and start building. Something simple (all I care about is a fireplace, hot tub and sauna!)
We hope everything is well with you!
Love, Kathie & Greg

Joy

Sit Right Down and Write Myself a Letter

If you've got the kind of penmanship that people envy, you can create a handwritten newsletter like this one and make it seem even more like a letter to a friend. The handwriting and the use of first person pronouns ("I" and "we") combine to give this simple newsletter a warm, personal touch.

🎔 🎔 🎔

"Sir, more than kisses, letters mingle souls. For, thus friends absent speak."

—John Donne
English poet

An observation for the 1st Christmas of the 90s:

Slipping into the 90s... or Where's the Enjoli Woman?

Remember the Enjoli Woman? (You know. The commercial of the voluptuous vamp vending perfume that's only shown around Christmas time... leaving you to believe that it's bought by men for women who never wear it. Has anyone ever smelled Enjoli? Have you asked, "That's a great perfume you're wearing. What is it?" and heard, "Oh, it's Enjoli, of course." Is it a cosmetic version of the pet rock and no one caught on?)

I've been waiting all season to see the Enjoli woman. I keep wondering, "Will they change her? Will she be more of a 90s type of gal?" If they update the commercial, it's the most important social change of the decade. It would mark the death of the woman who does it all.

So far, I've only seen Enjoli in a discount store's Christmas ad. "A $14.50 value for $7.95." I considered it a bad omen.

The Enjoli Woman of the 90s:
You can bring home the muffin,
Microwave it on low,
And watch me and the kids go, go, go,
'Cause I'm a woo-o-man, Enjoli.

I won't work 'til the kids are in school,
Take them to prodigy lessons, I'm no fool,
And if it's loving you want
You'll just have to wait in line.
'Cause I'm a woo-o-man, Enjoli.

For your one-hour-after-the-kids-are-asleep
woooman.

Where did the Enjoli woman go wrong? Granted, her message has several flaws by today's standards. Try bringing home the bacon and frying it up in a pan now. (Honey, what about my colester-all?) Having children and working until nine o'clock? Think of the glaring mothers in your play group. Don't try to pull over the concept of quality time on them. These women are pros.

Perhaps real Enjoli women never existed. Maybe men no longer buy the concept of the sizzling, work-all-day mom. The makers of Enjoli could always try being honest with men. Nah. Her new tune would never move bottles.

—Elaine
For my sister Laura who, no doubt,
misses the Enjoli woman too.

Tips for Creating Editorials

If many of your family and friends live nearby and are well-versed already in your news, consider sending an editorial-style newsletter instead. Pick a subject that's timely or near to your heart and send in out in letter format.

❑ Make it personal, maybe just about your family.

❑ Avoid extremely political or controversial topics unless your audience is uniform in its beliefs.

❑ If appropriate, use humor to lighten your message.

❑ Keep it short.

❑ Allow other family members to express their views.

❑ Write it in first person ("I" and "me") so it's obvious the thoughts are your own.

"For there is no friend like a sister

In calm or stormy weather;

To cheer one on the tedious way,

To fetch one if one goes astray,

To lift one if one totters down,

To strengthen whilst one stands."

—**Christina Rossetti**
English poet

1996

Greetings again from the family team;
This year's poem will have *firsts* as a theme.
If you have kids, then you know what feelings would be like;
When things happen, like Chelsea's first ride on a bike.
Or starting first grade, or that first lost-tooth look;
Beginning Brownies, or reading her first book.
She did them all! Plus Molli had her share—
First time in Mom's make-up, and she cut her own hair!
Played soccer, snapped her fingers, swang "high like the clouds!";
She was in her first wedding...a flower girl, and oh-so proud!
Anna started ~~walking~~ running, talking and had chicken pox to rub;
Fell in love with Barney — and fell clothed, head-first, into the tub!
There were other firsts for our family to share;
Like Holiday World, and Indy camping with Yogi Bear.
We built our first snow house, and bought our first sled to play;
Took all the kids sledding, for a week-long hour one day!
The usual "got snow in my gloves," with faces powdered and dotty;
And, you guessed it, the dreaded, "Daddy, I gotta poddy."
We were all gift bearers at mass...one of those Kodak moment scenes;
Went to a billion showers and gatherings, had a kids party for Halloween.
Tracey's *firsts* were a round of golf, and roller blading a while;
David's were less fun...painted the house and grouted tile.
Other activities meant that few days were clear;
Both of us landed on school boards this year.
David's still doing soccer, softball, Festival and Sunday school;
Tracey's leading Brownies, and sported the kids to the pool.
Probably no surprise to you, we saw Springsteen (on a stool);
We certainly miss the Boss, when the E-Street ruled!
It was another great year for our group of five;
Simply seems to get better every day we're alive.
I'm not sure "happier" is possible, for us these days;
We truly are thankful for what God sends our way.
The kids play "house" and "dolls" — like we used to do;
Learn to sing songs, dance, and share together, too.
Every night we tuck them in, and listen to their prayers;
We smile and think to ourselves...so thankful to be theirs.

We hope this season finds you as happy as can be;
And we ask God to bless you and your family.
Merry Christmas! Have a great '97!

Create a scrapbook for each of your children, grandchildren or nieces, nephews, etc., with each year's newsletter or collection of newsletters.

"Writing my holiday poem each year is a special time for me. I reflect on the year and let my memories guide the poem. Writing this for my own family and our friends puts me in the holiday spirit better than chestnuts roasting on an open fire!"

— David

A Holiday Newsletter with Poetic Flair

If you enjoy writing poetry, give a rhyming recap a try. Each year, David captures the year's highlights of his wife and three girls in poem format. The family has fun choosing matching shirts and posing for a cover shot that's reproduced and glued to the outside of a card. The poem is printed on the inside.

David's poetic style works because of his choice of simple words and descriptions of smile-spurring family scenes.

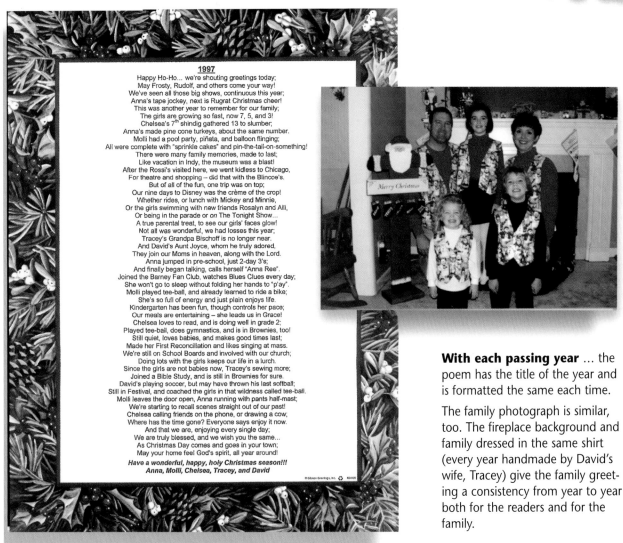

1997

Happy Ho-Ho... we're shouting greetings today;
May Frosty, Rudolf, and others come your way!
We've seen all those big shows, continuous this year;
Anna's tape jockey, next is Rugrat Christmas cheer!
This was another year to remember for our family;
The girls are growing so fast, now 7, 5, and 3!
Chelsea's 7th shindig gathered 13 to slumber;
Anna's made pine cone turkeys, about the same number.
Molli had a pool party, piñata, and balloon flinging;
All were complete with "sprinkle cakes" and pin-the-tail-on-something!
There were many family memories, made to last;
Like vacation in Indy, the museum was a blast!
After the Rossi's visited here, we went kidless to Chicago,
For theatre and shopping – did that with the Blincoe's.
But of all of the fun, one trip was on top;
Our nine days to Disney was the crème of the crop!
Whether rides, or lunch with Mickey and Minnie,
Or the girls swimming with new friends Rosalyn and Alli,
Or being in the parade or on The Tonight Show...
A true parental treat, to see our girls' faces glow!
Not all was wonderful, we had losses this year;
Tracey's Grandpa Bischoff is no longer near.
And David's Aunt Joyce, whom he truly adored,
They join our Moms in heaven, along with the Lord.
Anna jumped in pre-school, just 2-day 3's;
And finally began talking, calls herself "Anna Ree".
Joined the Barney Fan Club, watches Blues Clues every day;
She won't go to sleep without folding her hands to "p'ay".
Molli played tee-ball, and already learned to ride a bike;
She's so full of energy and just plain enjoys life.
Kindergarten has been fun, though controls her pace;
Our meals are entertaining – she leads us in Grace!
Chelsea loves to read, and is doing well in grade 2;
Played tee-ball, does gymnastics, and is in Brownies, too!
Still quiet, loves babies, and makes good times last;
Made her First Reconciliation and likes singing at mass.
We're still on School Boards and involved with our church;
Doing lots with the girls keeps our life in a lurch.
Since the girls are not babies now, Tracey's sewing more;
Joined a Bible Study, and is still in Brownies for sure.
David's playing soccer, but may have thrown his last softball;
Still in Festival, and coached the girls in that wildness called tee-ball.
Molli leaves the door open, Anna running with pants half-mast;
We're starting to recall scenes straight out of our past!
Chelsea calling friends on the phone, or drawing a cow;
Where has the time gone? Everyone says enjoy it now.
And that we are, enjoying every single day;
We are truly blessed, and we wish you the same...
As Christmas Day comes and goes in your town;
May your home feel God's spirit, all year around!

Have a wonderful, happy, holy Christmas season!!!
Anna, Molli, Chelsea, Tracey, and David

With each passing year ... the poem has the title of the year and is formatted the same each time.

The family photograph is similar, too. The fireplace background and family dressed in the same shirt (every year handmade by David's wife, Tracey) give the family greeting a consistency from year to year both for the readers and for the family.

Tips for Creating Great Poetry

❏ **Poetry doesn't have to rhyme.** Rhythm, imagery and word choice give poetry its power.

❏ **Avoid forced rhyme**. Most trouble comes from forced syntax to achieve the rhyme. *Her hair, it was gold. Her dress, it was old* is clumsy. An ambitious but misguided amateur poet once rhymed "obelisk" with "boggled by this."

❏ **Watch for clichéd rhymes**. In songs, if a line ends with "above," you can be certain the next will end in "love." Break those patterns with the help of a rhyming dictionary.

❏ **Listen to the rhythm**. Read your poem aloud—words should flow, and the rhythm should rise and fall naturally.

❏ **Let rhythm guide word choice**. "House" sounds different than "residence;" "listen" different than "hear."

❏ **Write several drafts**. Edit and cut mercilessly, but don't throw your old drafts away yet. There may be a line you want to resurrect.

Poems can be cute, fun, creative and imaginative. But they can also be awkward, annoying or maudlin. If you try writing a poem and it just isn't working, try a letter-style instead.

Merry Christmas from the Prairie

As I write this newsletter, we have four inches of snow on the ground and will probably have more before the week is over. It is pretty to look at, but it keeps us indoors far more than we are accustomed to. Our exercise program gets more creative—.as soon as the sun comes out and the wind is less than 10 mph, we go for it! Our children gave us a very handy weather station gizmo that gives us the temperature, wind velocity and direction, and wind chill factor. We put it to good use.

Jim and I are both fine. We have one and a half years until Jim retires from U.S. Filter and we can go back home. Our children are also fine. We have made several trips to St. Louis this year to see Elaine and Alex and grandkids, Alex (4) and Daniele (2). Elaine also makes it to Chicago on business now and then, so we see them quite often. Alex is waiting to hear the results of his medical school application, so we don't know if they will remain in St. Louis after August.

Laura and Jay planned such a nice family reunion for us in July. We rented two beach houses in Manzanita, Oregon, on the coast. All of our children and grandchildren and my mom and sister were there.

We miss our two grandkids Ross (9) and Dana (7) out in Moraga. We made two trips to see them, one last February when they had some days off school and another before school in September. Debbie was able to fly to Chicago in May to see us for a long weekend and Elaine brought the kids up from St. Louis at that time.

Raymond and Tiffany are expecting their first child in August. We were kidding them about the timing since we have five family birthdays in August, including both Tiffany's and Raymond's.

We celebrated our 40th wedding anniversary in September with a party with Debbie, Dennis, Ross and Dana, followed by a trip to the big island of Hawaii. One of the benefits of Jim's frequent commutes from New Jersey and Illinois to the West coast a few years ago is the accumulation of frequent flyer miles! Hopefully, we will have enough left for another over-seas trip after we retire.

We'd like to be going to the Rose Bowl this year to see Ohio State play, but we fear the demand for tickets among OSU alumni leave us out of the lottery. I'll be making a trip to Moraga the day after Christmas and stay until New Years. We have invited another former California family to spend Christmas with us. They have five kids and their mom, Chris, works with me.

Jim and I look forward to hearing from all of you and news of your families.

Before: Working with Your First Draft

After you write the first draft of your newsletter, go back over your work and look for:

❑ Detail to add to your news that helps make a personal connection.

❑ Detail that isn't necessary.

❑ Opportunities to add appropriate humor or personalization.

See the worksheets on page 100 and 101 of the Writing Tools section for assistance with writing and editing.

Merry Christmas *from the Prairie*

Dear Friends,

As I write, we have four inches of snow on the ground, with more on the way. It's pretty to look at, but it keeps us inside too much. We're adjusting from the warm California sun with a creative exercise program. As soon as the sun comes out and the wind is less than 10 mph, we go for it! Our children gave us a handy weather station gizmo that we put to good use.

Jim and I are both fine. We have one and a half years until Jim retires and we can go back home. I'm working at the Crusader Clinic, a non-profit clinic, in the lab. When we're not working, we enjoy volunteering at church, we are both active on several committees, and—weather permitting—landscaping the yard. We've also developed a new appreciation for basketball (Go Bulls!), but don't worry, fellow Buckeyes—our first love is still football.

Our children are also fine. We have made several trips to St. Louis this year to see Elaine and Alex and grandkids, Alex (4) and Daniele (2). It's been fun being so close geographically; Daniele is such a little lady now, and little Alex loves spending time with his grandfather in the workshop. Papa Alex is waiting to hear the results of his medical school application, so we don't know if they'll remain in St. Louis after August.

Laura and Jay planned such a nice family reunion for us in July. We rented two beach houses in Manzanita, Oregon, on the coast. All of our children and grandchildren and my mom and sister were there. Having that many people around was an adjustment at first, but everyone pitched in to make the trip a success. We enjoyed being able to take long walks on the beach and just spend time together.

We miss grandkids Ross (9) and Dana (7) in Moraga. We made two trips to see them, in February and September. They're growing up so fast. We got to see some of Ross's basketball games when we were there, and Dana (nicknamed "The Gazelle") is doing very well in track.

Raymond and Tiffany are expecting their first child in August. We have been kidding them about the timing since we have five family birthdays in August, including both Tiffany's and Raymond's.

We celebrated our 40th wedding anniversary in September with a party with Debbie, Dennis, Ross and Dana, followed by a trip to the big island of Hawaii. One of the benefits of Jim's traveling is the accumulation of frequent flyer miles!

We'd like to be going to the Rose Bowl this year to see Ohio State play, but we fear the demand for tickets among OSU alumni leave us out of the lottery. I'll be making a trip to Moraga the day after Christmas and will stay until New Year's. We've invited another former California family to spend Christmas with us. They have five kids and their mom, Chris, works with me. It'll be fun having a houseful of kids again.

Jim and I look forward to hearing from all of you and news of your families.

Love,
Carol

After: Out with the Old and In with the News

The newsletter to the left was changed to include:

❏ A salutation, "Dear Friends."

❏ A signature at the end.

❏ A more conversational writing style with the use of contractions.

❏ Memorable details (such as the nickname "Gazelle") to make it personal.

❏ A paper color that still looks festive but matches the "prairie" theme.

Include a snapshot along with the printed newsletter. There is no greater human connection on a page than through a photograph.

Chapter Five:
Computer-Generated News

A re your fingers happiest when tap dancing across a keyboard? Do you harbor a yearning to be a publisher? Do you like creating on a computer screen? If you want to use your home, school, work or library computer to create your newsletter, you're at the right place.

This chapter gives you ideas on how to create a beautiful computer-generated newsletter. You'll learn the basics of good publication design along with seeing where to find additional computer resources for papers and artwork. As a special bonus, pages 54 to 57 at the end of the chapter show how to create genealogy newsletters.

Before you start perusing the examples, take a moment to consider some of the benefits and some of the drawbacks of creating a professional-looking newsletter.

The benefits:
❏ Looks organized and well put together.
❏ Satisfies the demands of a more sophisticated reading public.
❏ May begin an interest in journalism and desktop publishing.
❏ May be the beginning of a business.

The drawbacks:
❏ Takes more time.
❏ The time you spend on design could be spent on better content.
❏ Takes more knowledge of good layout and typography.
❏ May get accidentally thrown away as junk mail.
❏ May look less personal.
❏ May look too "professional" and not as approachable.
❏ Requires more equipment and supplies.
❏ For classroom project, requires a computer lab.
❏ For small children, requires typing ability.

> ✾ ✾ ✾
>
> "The most impressive increase in responses came when I purchased (and finally learned how to use...and after upgrading my aging desktop computer) a scanner.
>
> The addition of pictures to the newsletter changed it from a collection of dates and names to real people."
>
> **—Walter Ayars, III**

(Above) Polly and Bob's "wall of newsletters."

Pattison Productions

JANUARY 1996

HAPPY NEW YEAR! Hope you have time for one more post-holiday letter from friends. The season went by much too fast for us.

✔ Our water saga continues. California's 50 year flood in January was disaster for us. For second time in two years we had two inches of water over our entire downstairs. Streets and storm drains overflowed with a vengeance. Didn't know our house was lowest on street. Now we do.

✔ Many hours were spent all through the year on cleanup of persistent problems from the two floods. Bob bore most of the brunt of this work.

✔ Elder care for two mothers continues, with Bob's mother (90) needing more and more. She made a major move in April into a facility with three meals a day. Unfortunately the first day there she took a fall, resulting in fractures to the spine. Getting used to the new environment went very slowly, with much difficulty.

✔ We visited Polly's mother (96) in the desert as often as possible. She's in great health except for her memory. She can still take in most phone calls, mail and visits.

✔ Biopsy surgery for Polly in April thankfully proved negative, but recovery took much longer than expected.

✔ A springtime business/pleasure trip to Oregon and Washington at height of blooming season helped us understand why Northwesterners put up with all that rain. Mother Nature really turns on a spring spectacular!

✔ Two visits to Colorado kept us caught up with granddaughter Tasha (age four) and her parents, Lorinda and Jim, and also gave us time with Carol Ann and Gene.

✔ Getting on-line in August, with help of nephew Doug Beal, opened up an awesome new world. Learned to write even shorter and tighter, because of "email." Phone bills to family steadily decrease – contact with business world speeds up. Reach us at pollypatt@aol.com if you're online.

✔ Polly's training is slowing down as she heads for retirement. A reorganization of her major three-day course will demand new creativity in teaching. A major client will market her Advanced Newsletter Design once again. She's still working on her fifth book and teaching in UK yearly.

✔ Christmas consisted of a busy and very unusual reunion with Bob's family from Colorado, Washington, the high desert as well as the low desert.

We have enjoyed cards and news from so many friends this season. We wish you joy and continued effectiveness in 1996.

All Shapes and Sizes

Newsletter design expert Polly Pattison experiments with different newsletter sizes each year in her *Pattison Productions*. To the left is a letter-sized sheet cut in half and written in skinny checklist-style then folded to postcard size. Above is Polly's postcard version.

For her studio in her new home, she framed 21 newsletters that she has done over the years. Each one has a different format and color. "It makes a nice memory wall in my office," says Polly. "The early ones were all done on my typewriter. Only a few people really noticed that I was changing the format each year but some were inspired with ideas for their own holiday newsletters."

Pattison Productions

CHRISTMAS 1996

Are you surprised at our new address?
We hope not, after our last two newsletters with tales of the water problems in our CA house. In fact, you probably wondered why we stayed so long. We wanted to get out of the area for some time. A real estate broker brought us a buyer in late February, we disclosed all, and had an offer in five days. What a big decision. We were out in one month! And the house wasn't even on the market. Did we ever scramble.

Fast decisions about where to relocate
We had looked in many areas of the West for several years, coming back again and again to the beauty and small-town feeling of St. George, Utah. The area seemed to have what we needed, particularly a nice retirement community for Bob's mother, and good medical services. We moved two households in six weeks, with wonderful assistance from Barb and Don Libby. Her California condo sold the same week ours did.

Two hours north of Las Vegas, the St. George weather is mild and the scenery outstanding. Very close to some of our country's most beautiful national parks, it's a photographer's paradise. Joining a local camera club has helped us find new friends. There's lots to do. While not easy to make such a radical change, we feel we are on an exciting new course. We are now one day closer to both Lorinda's family, and to Carol Ann and Gene.

Elder care continues as a big part of our life
Bob's mother had a severe stroke in October so we are now learning the ropes of an excellent rehab facility. It is fortunate Polly took time off from teaching for the last part of the year. We bought a lot in September, broke ground in November, look forward to moving in by July 4th, after the joys and tribulations of building our own home. We'll have a beautiful view and a spare room, so put Southern Utah on your itinerary for a future vacation. We'd love to see you! Happy 1997.

CHRISTMAS 1997

Pattison Productions

IN THIS ISSUE:
• Getting closer to nature
• Polly's Mom moves to Minnesota
• Losing a loved one is never easy

Living on the edge!

We're folks who have lived where we couldn't see the sun rise, seldom saw the sun set. It is a fantastic experience to live where now we actually can **see** the weather! While washing dishes, yet, at the kitchen sink.

Our new house on the hill overlooks ridges, valleys and cliffs, with the mountains of Zion National Park in the distance and a 10,000 foot mountain to the north.

Regardless of what kind of weather it is, it still seems magic for us. Rainbows, gold-lined clouds, magnificent sunrises and spectacular sunsets over the vermilion cliffs give us a moving show every day.

We feel very fortunate to live in a small town where we can jump in the car and be in the wilderness – or at the mall – in about five minutes. We are enjoying getting acquainted with new people and new surroundings and gradually settling into our new house, which was finished in August.

The local Camera Club has particularly broadened our horizons and given Bob a chance to practice his excellent photographic skills. After years of working in black and white or video, he is now back into shooting color scenics. He also hopes to get his dark room set up in the new year.

Thought she'd never quit?

Polly is enjoying a much quieter schedule these days, not really of her own making. The market for her kind of training has slowed down. Perhaps this is partly due to the internet frenzy in which communicators have to master the internet, intranets, create homepages or electronic newsletters. Editors have no time for seminars?

Or could it be due to the abundance of good books out there on newsletters and design, which has given editors enough knowledge so they no longer need training? Polly's last gig of the year was perhaps her nicest assignment – training over 100 editors at the Ford International Newsletter Conference in Dearborn MI.

Theone moves to Minnesota

Polly and her siblings have long felt that their mother should be closer to one of the family. After a long search, the right assisted living facility was located, just five minutes from brother David's home and office.

In October David, Polly and Carol Ann's husband Gene went to California to help Theone make the big move. While Gene packed up all the things that couldn't go on the plane, Dave, Polly and Theone made the big trip by air.

She now is adjusting well to her new surroundings, and participating in events in the care center as best she can. She has a private room, a beautiful view overlooking a pond, trees and ducks, with visits from Dave, Audrey or grandson Doug quite frequently. At 98, she still surprises us all with her unexpected wit and her amazingly good health.

We say good-bye to Bob's mom

In October, a disabling stroke hit which meant we had to move Alice from her lovely retirement apartment to a nursing facility. Medicare provided considerable assistance with all kinds of therapy, and the care in the facility was exceptional.

One day Polly asked her "Doesn't this

all get a bit boring?" She cheerfully replied that she loved having people in and out, and there was always something to do. This is another side to life in a nursing home, in contrast to her sedentary and often lonely life alone in an apartment.

But a second stroke hit her hard in February, and that was it. She tried bravely but nothing worked. Her granddaughter, Lorinda, and great-granddaughter Tasha arrived just before she died on March 15. Grandson John, Beverly, Carol Ann and Gene, along with neighbors and friends gathered for a memorial in St. George.

Then we drove her down to Forest Lawn Cemetery in Southern California for burial next to Bob's father and others in her family. Returning to the California she loved so much gave a fitting closure to her life. We miss her a lot and are thankful for the many joys of her 90 years.

If I-15 is on your route to anywhere, stop in and see us. Here's our latest photos so you will recognize us and our new home. We're in the high desert, just two hours north of Las Vegas.

[handwritten note] we thought I was retired then I got 2 emails this week for training dates. A woman from Ohio wants one on one training in my home new year's week. The other is a convention for American Psychiatry Assoc. in Florida in Feb. Just when I was enjoying putting up wall paper! We'll see! merry Christmas, Polly & Bob

[handwritten caption] my computer office is on front. All other rooms have views on back, over the walk-out basement. Bob is building a video...

Desktop Publishing Tips from Polly Pattison

Publication design trainer Polly Pattison follows her own rules of good design to achieve the professional yet warm look of the *Pattison Productions*. Her tips:

❏ Keep the format simple. The three-column design above is easy to read.

❏ Keep articles short. Include three to four articles per page.

❏ Use no more than three fonts—one for the text, one for headlines and a third for lists or other information that's printed in smaller type.

❏ Give your newsletter warmth and quality by choosing a good paper.

❏ Use professionally designed graphics and clip art.

❏ For an ongoing newsletter, take the time to design a professional nameplate (the area where the name of the newsletter appears).

For help with naming your newsletter, see pages 94 to 98.

Season's Readings
Special Holiday Greetings We Hope Yule Enjoy

A holiday newsletter? Yes! We think this is a novel way to send holiday greetings to our family, friends, and business associates. It lets us express more than we can on a card and it is a reflection of who we are and what we do. We hope you enjoy reading it and find your own way of expressing what's in your heart this Holiday Season.

When the spirit of Peace becomes a part of our lives, every day will be like those of the Holiday Season and every night will hold the promise of a bright and warm sunrise.

The Holiday Season is the shining festival of the unselfish...the homecoming of the spirit...the glorification of all that is good.

For Our Family And Friends

As we rapidly approach "the season" we reflect on yet another year. Not only did Les think the baseball season was a little shorter than usual, but it seems as if the year flew by a bit quicker. The only way I can tell it isn't quite over yet is because I haven't quite reached my billionth editing job for Calendar 1995. Hold the phone–I think I'm getting close.

Les is still Zepping along. This April it will be 20 years at Zep–20 years since he gave up playing with drums and started selling them.

We gained a family member this year with the marriage of our son Shane to Rachelle. Although they met on an airplane going to Jamaica–their relationship is not "up in the air."

Brittany is an angel...when she's sleeping! A 1st Honors student in the fourth grade, she plays basketball and enjoys activities with her Girl Scout troop. She appears on the front of a children's makeup package, and costarred in the series premiere of "In The Name Of Love" for the Lifetime Channel.

Our dogs, Gretel and Nadia, insist upon sitting in my office chair with me while I work. After dropping off Brittany at school each morning, Gretel anticipates her daily fix of bacon from the Hardee's crew.

Overall we've had a wonderful year, good health, good fortune, and each other–if we never do any better we'll all be quite thankful.

We wish all our friends and family good health and happiness–not just for the '95 Holiday Season–but for all of '96 and beyond.

Imagine all the people...imagine if you can...living life in Peace.

For Our Business Associates

We live in trying times, nothing seems to be the way it used to be. Job stress, mergers, downsizing, restructuring, competition, wage cuts, price cuts, are just some of the concerns we must all deal with in our business day.

Now more than ever, in order to survive and thrive in the business world it is crucial to build better, more personal business relationships. We need to communicate more effectively with each other and nothing communicates more effectively than the message that says "I Care." Tell others you care and you will find new and better ways to strengthen the business ties that bind you to your customers and prospects.

Thank you for caring about us, and thank you for the confidence and trust you have placed in us. We look forward to continuing our successful association with you.

Let the sounds of the Holiday Season echo in your heart all year long.

How To Help Yourself Through The Holidays

1. Shop early.
2. Sit down with your family and decide what you want to do for the Holiday Season and then let relatives and friends know.
3. There is no right or wrong way to handle the holidays.
4. Keep in mind the feelings of your children or family members and make the holiday season as joyous as possible for them.
5. Do something different for someone else, such as volunteering, asking some-

...that is not really... to make time are to cancel regular... like lessons or appointments for a few weeks, or to schedule "Family Day" when everyone takes a day off from other commitments. Slowing down, doing less, spending more time together... sounds good. Sounds like a real holiday!

How To Care For The First Plant Of The Holiday Season — The Poinsettia

As a symbol of the Holiday Season, the poinsettia is a completely American development. These plants were brought to this country in 1836 by our first Minister to Mexico, Dr. Joel R. Poinsett, and were thus named after him. As it grew in the wild, the poinsettia was a wild, smelly weed, but cultivation has produced the lovely flamboyant flower we know today.

Poinsettias are sensitive, they drop leaves if placed in a warm or cool draft, or in a too warm or too cool room. Water soil thoroughly when necessary and avoid drafts. Be sure to...

...loosen the foil around the pot to let the soil drains properly.

Children's Artwork As Wrap For Holiday Gifts

...feel guilty about discarding your...'s old accumulated artwork, or...urting their feelings when they...r their beloved masterpieces haven't...ved, here's a way to deal with all that...ity and allow your budding artists to...with pride.

...fter displaying artwork, fold and tuck it...in a wrapping paper box. Then use the...wrap around gifts of friends and family...bers. And if you run out of homemade...pping, just get the kids busy and have...m make some more.

Custom Of Christmas Cards

The first Christmas card was created in 1843 by John Calcott Horsley, an English illustrator. It resembled a postcard and showed a large family enjoying Christmas together. The message on the card read, "A Merry Christmas And A Happy New Year To You." Smaller drawings on the cards showed people helping the needy. The first Christmas cards manufactured in the United States were made in 1875 by Louis Prang, a German-born Boston printer.

Enjoying the May wedding reception...
Maralah, Les, Rachelle, Shane, Brittany

Maralah

Photo Label in Lombard, Illinois, (800) 323-0776, can transfer your photos to stickers.

Keeping the Spirit of the Season Inclusive

Season's Readings is a great example of using cross cultural graphics in a holiday newsletter. Because Maralah is Christian and her husband is Jewish, their list of friends and family includes both religions. This newsletter shows both the Nativity and the Menorah and refers to the season and the holidays.

This newsletter was printed on a color laser printer. The color photograph of the family is a sticker affixed to the page. (See left for information on photo stickers.)

No Need to Choose Between a Card and a Newsletter

You can do both. This card folded over to create a cover with "Merry Christmas, Happy New Year" and the back with "You Know You're a Parent…" This created the feeling of a card with room for news along with room for a personalized message under the page "Dear Friends & Family." It was mailed in matching card-sized envelopes from Paper Direct (see page 108).

March 7-8, 1998
Victoria, British Columbia

Surprise Birthday Celebration

A special surprise for mom's 70th birthday is underway! A weekend of fun in Victoria, B.C. is planned that includes all sisters. There will be plenty of time to shop in the quaint 19th century shops. You can find almost anything English ~ woolens and tartan plaids, bone china, family crests, toffee and other English delights. There's the Crystal Gardens, Chinatown, Craigdarroch Castle and the world renowned floral displays at Butchart

Gardens. The famous English High Tea is still served daily in the elegant ivy-covered Empress Hotel. Dinner reservations have been made at IL Terrazzo, featuring Northern Italian cooking with wood-oven specialties, pastas and fresh seafood. The restaurant is located off Waddinton Alley, beside Market Square, a very quaint location.

BC Ferries and WA State Ferries will Whisk Us Away!

We will take the Tsawwassen-Nanaimo ferry to Victoria. It's a ferry port, just across the U.S. Canadian Border. Our ferry trip will be approximately 1 hour, 35 minutes. We leave Bellingham at 10am to take the 11am ferry, arriving in Victoria at about 12:35pm. Cost roundtrip is about $23 Canadian (appprox. $17 U.S.).

The plan is for Terri bring mom via a Washington State Ferry from Seattle to Victoria. She won't know what is in store for her. We of course should arrive just before they do, and surprise mom at the Empress Hotel lobby, where we will have reservations for afternoon tea at 2:00pm.

Our plan is to return on the 5pm ferry arriving back in Bellingham at around 7:30pm. If you need to make arrangements to return home on that Sunday evening via Seattle airport, let us know ASAP and we can take an earlier ferry back.

Victoria is best known as the capital city of British Columbia. It's located 85 miles northwest of Seattle. Our ferry voyage will take us through some of the most beautiful waters and islands in the world; considered by many visitors to be a highlight of their trip. Victoria's unique character is deeply rooted in its 150 year history.

Empress Hotel, Victoria, B.C.

Empress Hotel will be Home Base for Party

As a gift to mom, dad has offered to pick up the rooms for our weekend gala. The Empress is part of the Canadian Pacific Hotels. Built in 1908, the Empress is poised on the water's edge, in the center of the city's recreational and business district. It is one of the few remaining stately hotels in North America. Styled in the grand European tradition it contains all the amenities one would expect to find in today's contemporary hotels. Each room will include a full buffet breakfast for two on Sunday morning and incentive coupon books for over 40 of Victoria's most loved stores! Some of the discounts are for Roger's Chocolates, Munro's Books and the Royal British Columbia Museum.

Party Goers to Surprise Jeanne

This will be great surprise for mom when she's met by all of us at the Empress Hotel in Victoria, B.C. The big surprise will be ... to be with mom as we celebrate ...aeleen, coming from St. Louis, ... in the late fall that "something" was going to be planned for mom's birthday. She was ecstatic when she got the news of our March outing. Sister-in-law Sue and daughter, Kelly will be en route

from Provo, Utah; not easy his time of year. It's exciting to think about all of us being together for the first time and on a special occasion to surprise mom. Since this is a month before her birthday, she won't suspect a thing!

-daughter
Kelly

" Eaton Girls"

Itinerary - Saturday 3/7

7:15am - Leave Bellingham by Car
9am - Ferry to Victoria
10:30am - Arrive Victoria
11:30am - Empress Hotel Check-in
12:30pm - Tea at Empress Hotel
2:00pm - Free Time til Dinner
8pm - Dinner at IL Terrazzo
? - Free Time after Dinner

Itinerary - Sunday 3/8

9am - Buffet Breakfast
11am-4pm - Free Time
1pm - Hotel Check-out
5pm - Ferry Home
6:30pm - Drive to Bellingham
7:30pm - Arrive Bellingham

Time for Tea, Gathering Steam...

"These newsletters were made while organizing a surprise 70th birthday party for our mother. They were printed back to back on heavy off-white bond paper. I mailed them with Mary Engelbreit teapot stickers and 'time for tea' stamps on matching colored envelopes.

"The first newsletter went to my immediate family and my aunt, after we had invited them by phone.

"Once the newsletters were received, several first cousins wanted to come, too, after seeing how fun it would be. So, a week before the trip, I did a second newsletter, announcing the additional attendees and gave all the final details (see next page)."

Quick Facts

CANADIAN CURRENCY
Canadian currency, like U.S. money, is in dollars and cents. One dollar and two dollar denominations are coins, while all other dollar denominations are paper currency. International visitors, including US residents, should be aware of currency exchange rates. Visitors are encouraged to purchase a small amount of Canadian dollars before arriving. While U.S. cur-

rency is accepted at most Victoria businesses, exchange rates vary at the till. Most major credit cards can be used in Canada, and traveler's checks are universally accepted.

CANADA CUSTOMS & IMMIGRATION
Citizens or permanent residents of the United States require a birth or baptismal certificate, voter's regis-

tration card, or passport to enter Canada. A drivers license is not accepted as proof of citizenship. All persons entering Canada must fill our a declaration for Canada Customs.

CLIMATE
Victoria is located in a "sub-Mediterranean" climate zone and has moderate weather year-round. Average temperature in March should be low to mid 50°F.

What Tea at the Empress Really Means

It may be an English custom, but Victoria has perfected the ritual of afternoon tea, that totally civilized "almost-a-Meal". The menu has recently changed at the Empress, but tea service typically includes delicacies such as English crumpets or scones, fresh berries and Devon cream, finger sand-

wiches and cake. A special slice of a decorated piece of cake will be given to mom as a birthday treat.
When making the reservation, I was told that the dress code was "smart casual". Anticipated price per person is $20 Canadian (approx $14 U.S.). Don't eat lunch first... you'll be sorry!

March 7-8, 1988
Victoria, British Columbia   Part II

Surprise to Happen at Tea

To date, we are almost certain that mom does not suspect a thing. Mom and Dad have had plans to travel to Washington for a speaking engagement in Bellingham on Tuesday, March 10th. To make the trip worthwhile, they planned to spend a week, visiting with Terri's family in Redmond and then up to Bellingham to see Judy, Jan and Cindy's families. We thought this was an opportune time to surprise Mom with a birthday trip to Victoria. On a phone conversation with Terri last week, mom was asked if she wanted to join Terri on a weekend at the Empress Hotel in Victoria. Terri told her some story about going for some odd reason, and that the offer would expire in early March. Part of the guise was, that since mom was coming up with dad for his speaking engagement, why didn't she join Terri on the trip (and for whatever reason....Mike couldn't

go). Dad, in on the trick, said what a good idea it was...that mom should go. So, the stage was set. She thinks that she and Terri are getting away for the weekend. Our plan, as mentioned before, is to meet up at the Empress tea room, where we have reservations for the 12:30pm seating. We will have to try and avoid mom and Terri in the hotel lobby, as we may arrive within minutes of each other. Plan to dress in what you will wear to tea, as our rooms may not be ready for check-in. Attire is "smart casual" for the tea room. I was told that dress jeans are OK, but tennis shoes not good.

Mom to Arrive Via Victoria Clipper

VICTORIA CLIPPER
SEATTLE VICTORIA
Since 1986

Terri will bring mom on the Victoria Clipper sailing from Seattle. Mom doesn't know this, but Terri has only bought a one-way ticket for her, since she will return to Bellingham with us on our ferry. Dad will have driven to Bellingham that Sunday afternoon.
If you have a flight out on Sunday night, you will need to return with Terri on this ferry line into Seattle. Departure ___ ___oria is 6pm, arriving in Seattle at 8:30pm. ___ ___d there is a Duty Free

shop with a wide array of merchandise and Clipper gifts. There is taxi transportation for travelers going on to SeaTac airport, a short 1/2 hour ride. If you need to return with Terry on this ferry, you can book your reservation with the toll free number shown on page two. You need to request the taxi voucher at that time. Or, if you have an early flight out Monday morning you can take this ferry and stay overnight at Terri's (she has a really early business flight out of the same airport).

B.C. FERRIES

d this is a big ferry (see picture above) and there is breakfast currency, but if you have already planned to exchange money, Canadian dollars, just in case. The crossing is one hour, 35 t 1/2 hour car trip from the ferry dock. The scary part is that are pulling into town. Oh-Oh.

Kris (Jim's daughter)   Sherrie (Dan's Wife)   Sherry (Mike's Wife)

Party Grows to Include Nieces

It is with great excitement that we have more surprises in store for mom. Kris McNab, Uncle Jim's daughter, is flying up from Sunnyvale, California. Kris is an insurance company field adjuster and has been anxious to meet her cousins for a long time. Sherrie Heton and Sherry Heton (no mistake ~ they have similar names) will be joining us from Ballwin, Missouri. They are married to mom's nephews Danny and Mike and, naturally, are daughter-in-laws of Aunt Raeleen. We are anxious to meet our cousins (cousins in law?) and get to know each other after so many years. Should be fun.

Trip Cost Estimates

A few of us thought it would be easier to pay for group activities together and, after the trip, send out a little bill to each person for their share. We combined the cost of the ferry for everyone and divided it by ten of us. Sorry, my original ferry estimate was only a one way trip; I didn't use round trip costs. If you're going to return on the Clipper to Seattle with Terri, you'll need to purchase an additional one way ticket (they take credit cards).

Estimates based on group sharing & splitting tab:
• Ferry $30 (includes two cars and mom's tickets)
• Tea $18-19 (includes tip...not sure about tax)
• Room   -0- (dad is treating)
• Dinner   Moderate Pricing (we can split 10 ways?

Your presence on this trip is mom's gift, so please don't feel like you have to bring something.

Victoria Clipper

If you need to get to SeaTac for a late Sunday night or early Monday morning flight you will want to take the Vitoria Clipper. Terry will be returning on this ferry and you can ride with her. The Clipper leaves Victoria at 6pm and arrives in Seattle around 8:30pm. A 1/2 hour taxi ride will get you to the airport by 9pm. Cost one way is approximately $54.

Handi Numbers

Victoria Clipper (Ferry back to Seattle) 1-800-888-2535
Empress Hotel 1-800-441-1414
Jan Heton 605-555-8150
Judy Heton 360-555-5811
Terri Heton 425-555-8936
Cindy Heton 360-555-2536
Sue Heton 801-555-9646
Raeleen Heton 314-5553937
Sherry Heton 314-555-8677
Sherrie Heton 314-555-1869
Kris Heton 408-555-3755

Finalized Itineraries

Itinerary - Saturday 3/7
7:00am - Leave Bellingham by Car
9:00am - Ferry to Victoria
10:30am - Arrive Victoria, drive to hotel
11:00am - Empress Hotel check-in
12:30pm - Tea at Empress Hotel
2:00-7:00pm - Free Time til Dinner
8:00pm - Dinner at IL Terrazzo
? - Free Time after Dinner

Itinerary - Sunday 3/8
9:00am - Buffet Breakfast at Hotel
11:00am-4:00pm - Free Time
1:00pm - Possible Hotel check-out
4:00pm - Leave Victoria for Ferry
5:00pm - Ferry Home
6:30pm - Drive to Bellingham
7:30pm - Arrive Bellingham

Shuttle from Seattle to Bellingham

Cost: $29 one way ✤ $52 round trip
If you want to take a shuttle from the airport directly to Bellingham airport, call me to help make your reservation or figure out details. Could save $$ versus a car rental. The shuttle leaves SeaTac Airport every two hours from 9am to 11pm and goes back to SeaTac every two hours from 3am-7pm. Reservations are not necessary. At the airport go from baggage claim to door #26 and board the "Airporter Shuttle" with destination to the Bellingham Airport (approx. 2hr trip).

Time for Tea, the Whistle Blows...

"As you will note, we have family from Utah, Missouri, California and Washington State. Many of us had never met, or it had been 20 to 25 years since we had last seen each other. The newsletter helped break the ice by giving information and photos in advance.

"My mother never knew about the newsletters or the planning— we surprised her in Victoria, British Columbia, at the Empress Hotel reception lobby.

"The family has asked me to think about a quarterly newsletter, with items, articles, etc. submitted by everyone who wants to join in."
—Janice

❦ ❦ ❦
Ideas for What to List on Calendars:

- ❑ Birthdays (how old?)
- ❑ Graduations (from what grade, or what degree?)
- ❑ Weddings
- ❑ Confirmations
- ❑ Bar mitzvahs
- ❑ Baptisms
- ❑ Wedding anniversaries (how many years?)
- ❑ Business anniversaries (how many years?)
- ❑ Anniversaries of deaths
- ❑ Due dates for babies
- ❑ Photos
- ❑ Reminder dates (taxes, etc.)
- ❑ Reunion dates
- ❑ Reunion registration deadlines
- ❑ Parties

Communicate with "Refrigerator Journalism"

The desired spot for any newsletter (family, neighborhood, school or other) is on the family refrigerator. The best way to get this treasured spot is by designing a calendar. Family calendars such as the one above from the *Daoust Family Newsletter* keep members connected and supporting each other on birthdays, anniversaries, anniversaries of deaths, graduations and other important dates.

Handy software, such as the Calendar Creator programs listed in the Publishing Tools section on page 107, make calendar creation easy. Under the calendar or close by, preview upcoming important dates.

❧ ❧ ❧
If you mail the newsletter as a self-mailer, do not staple it shut. Most people will open the newsletter without use of a staple remover and will rip up the top (or more) in the process. Use tape, wafer seals or colorful stickers instead.

Mailing in an Envelope Versus Without

Some newsletters are folded and mailed on their own and others are mailed in an envelope.

The advantages of an envelope:

❑ Newsletters arrive in better condition.

❑ You can include more news in the newsletter.

❑ You can put other items such as photos in the envelope.

The drawbacks:

❑ An envelope with a computer-printed label may get tossed as junk mail.

❑ The extra weight of the envelope may increase postage costs.

❑ It takes more time to stuff envelopes and they add to the cost.

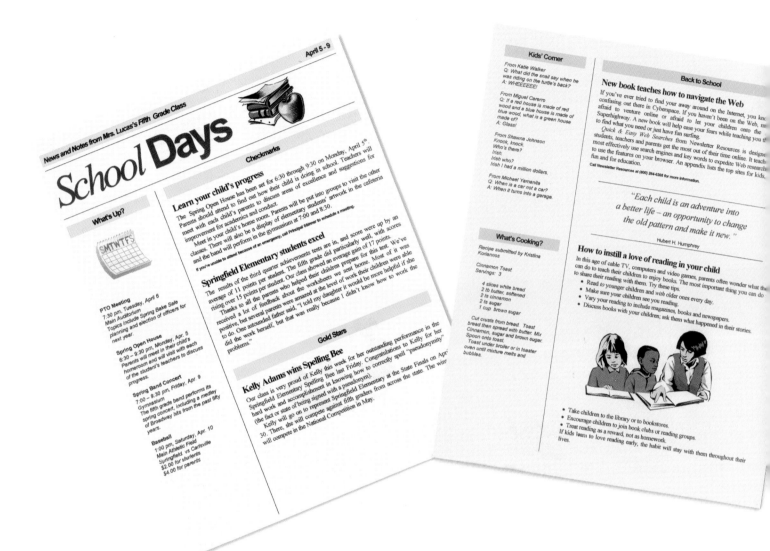

Experience the Wonders of Word Processing

As computers have become more and more powerful, so has word processing software. You can create columns, use colors and import graphics using software such as Microsoft Word. The newsletter above used one of the MS-Word templates from the book *Quick and Easy Newsletters*, listed in the Publishing Tools section on page 104.

This classroom project includes general news from the school, articles by kids and class news. Once the original layout has been created, subsequent issues are easy to put together by cutting and pasting text and graphics.

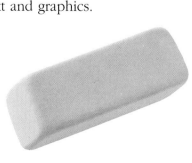

NEWS FOR and ABOUT MEMBERS of the BONNEY CLAN • NOVEMBER 1997

THE BONNEY BUGLE

96 Bonneys gathered in Colorado Springs for reunion of '97

This summer's gathering sparked the largest attendance in our 59-year history of reunions. This year a few attended for only one day, but most stayed the full three days.

Nearly one third of those attending came from the Clarence clan. All of Faith's children and grandchildren attended, and also all of Janet's children and grandchildren. That was historic. Nearly all of Alma, Wilma

Recalling other reunions

The march of time is irresisible, says Warren, one of our senior cousins.

A 1938 get-together prior to Grandma Elizabeth Bonney's death saw the "older" generation plan the informal event at the homestead. Polly, Rachel and Bonney Hallman were the youngest juveniles. Glen and Naomi, among others, were the essence of sophistication as teenagers, while the bratty club saw Brian, Carol Ann, Camden and Warren underfoot.

Auntie Wim was at home on the homestead. She was 47. Fern reigned as the eldest sister at 49. Clarence, down on the corner, was a 58-year-old farmer.

So far, the elder cousins' generation have organized most of the reunions. The torch has been formally passed to the next generation to organize the year 2000 reunion. Let's give Beth and her committee all the support we can.

and Theone's clans were there as well..

There was lots to do for all ages, planned by our creative program committee of Lyndon, Beth and Doug. The water slide on Sunday proved extremely popular, even though it was a bit nippy. T-shirt ty-dying went on all weekend, till the "wearing" Sunday night. Thanks Beth, Bonney and crew. And thanks to Kathy Thomas, Ken Sharp and Curt for the marvelous sing-along Saturday night.

Thanks also go to Warren and Lolly who helped everything run smoothly.

Gene and Carol Ann Francis, reunion organizers, seemed to have thought of everything. They reported nearly $10,000 changed hands during registration. Gene was amazed at the family turnout and he let us all know how much it means to him to be part

Reunion 2000 midwest site is set

Reunion chair for our next gathering is Beth Eash, granddaughter of Aunt Alma. She has reserved The Amigo Centre, a camp near Sturgis, Michigan, 20 miles north of the Indiana border.

For Bonney history buffs, the reunion site will be held less than 25 miles from Coldwater, MI where Grandpa George Bonney was born.

"This is an awesome and peaceful place," says Beth. "It's on a lake, with a beach, paddle boats, pontoon rides and there is lots to do. [...] a huge gym, there's b[...] leyball, ping pong, foo[...] side there's space for ten[...] a playground for the [...] can gather around the [...] place in the evenings."

of this clan, when he gave an impromptu but moving talk at the family business meeting Sunday.

"Holding reunions seems to be an exploding industry in the U.S.", he said after the reunion. "It makes me feel optimistic about our country, and is a positive comment on American life."

This reunion was different from past gatherings. Remember the massive food preparations for each meal in the Thomas house in 1975, when we did it ourselves? Remember the separate dorm facilities for men and women in Iowa in '82? The communal bathrooms in the Black Hills in 1993? Now we've graduated to rooms for two-four, with first-class food and minimum work. We can have it all – for a price! But wait till you hear the good news about Reunion 2000 prices!

"The best thing about our reunions," Beth says, "is to see all the younger ones connecting and getting to know each other."

Because Sturgis is in the heart of Amish country, Beth and her team hope to take us all to a traditional Amish country luncheon and an historic tour of the area Saturday.

The camp has every modern convenience, the food is excellent, and BEST OF ALL, the price will be approximately $100 less per person than

> "The best thing about our reunions," Beth says, "is seeing all the younger ones connecting and getting to know each other."

Message from Reunion Planning Expert, Tom Ninkovich

"The story of our family is perhaps the most valuable possession we have. It tells us where we've been so that we may steer a better course toward the future. It explains where we've come from so that we can more easily accept ourselves and relax into our lives. It gives us a sense of belonging as we see where and how we fit into the fabric of our family and of our society.

"The main job of a family newsletter editor is to impart the joy and wisdom of the family story. The printed page allows us to return again and again, hopefully to clearer understanding, as our own individual stories change and we gain newer insights. This can be done in many ways such as through poetry, photos, cartoons, puzzles, riddles, jokes, and of course, stories. But the shape, form and typestyles of newsletters also convey meaning—and much more meaning than most people realize."

—**Tom Ninkovich**, author of *Family Reunion Handbook*

For resources for family reunions, see page 104 of Publishing Tools.

ŏ ŏ ŏ

"I hated history in
school because it
was memorization
of names and
dates...not *why*. I
became interested in
history when I
owned an 1881
brick mansard
roofed home and
was involved in the
Lancaster County
Historical Society.

Later I took up the
search for our family
tree which my father
had begun. While
researching, I
became the organiz-
er of the Ayars
Reunion. It was a lot
of work but the mes-
sages of apprecia-
tion from those who
attended (and some
who could not)
made such an
impression that I
conceived the idea
of a family newslet-
ter... *Ayars Heirs*.

I enjoy the excite-
ment of the hunt—
opening up a fat
envelope of 'long
lost Ayars' and link-
ing up Ayars who
have lost touch with
ancestors. Readers
are also apprecia-
tive to have some-
thing to hand down
to their kids."

—**Walter Ayars III**

Photos and news of family
dwellings from *Ayars Heirs*.

Tips for Genealogy Newsletters from Experienced Editors

❏ Date, organize and file information as soon as it comes in. Make files for each issue or for standard columns in each issue. —Bette Butcher Topp

❏ Include the volume number, title, editor and address on every page. If someone finds your newsletter in a library, photocopies only one page, they have the contact information. —Bette Butcher Topp

❏ Consecutively number the pages. It makes it much easier to compile a master index. —Carolyn Weidner

❏ Be persistent in asking for submissions. —Larry Hamilton

❏ Do not expect to make money on a genealogical newsletter. Be pre-pared to give away more than you will receive. —Lynne D. Miller

❏ Schedule production times for your slack time periods. For two years, I produced an issue before Christmas. I later shifted to January. This made production much more enjoyable. —Cynthia L. Leet

❏ Start the next issue just after finishing the last. —Cynthia L. Leet

❏ Don't do a newsletter unless you have lots of information to impart and lots of time to devote to it. I was a history major and enjoy research and writing. It satisfies my need for both. —Joan Marie Meyering

❏ Don't give up at first. —Carolyn Weidner

The Dean Road

Sanctioned by the 7th Baron Kilmarnock, Alastair Ivor Gilbert Boyd
Chief of the Boyd Family

VOL. 11 NO. 38	1988-1998	JAN/1998

PRESIDENT:	Donald Boyd Mellen	TREASURER:	Allison B.Wikle
V. PRESIDENT:	David Drummond Boyd	SEC/EDITOR:	Richard G. Boyd
CO-EDITORS:	Lauren Beebe & Cal Boyd	GENEALOGIST:	Calvin Boyd

NON-PROFIT   ISSN 1087-223X

Visit the Boyd Clan Web pages at: Http://www.swgroup.com/Boyd/
Join the Boyd Clan List (BCL)   Boyd-L@Rootsweb.com
The Dick Institute, Kilmarnock Castle: 106111,647@Compuserve.com

PENKILL CASTLE LOOTED

Penkill Castle, unfortunate victim of one man's greed is located near Girvan, south of Glasgow which is en route to Stranraer Ferry that takes travellers to Ireland (it passes Kilmarnock) where Adam Boyd, first laird of Penkill and first of the Boyd's to inhabit the place (1532) lived and raised his family. Generations of Boyds lived and died there.

Spencer Boyd the 13th Laird died without issue in 1865. (see Vol 4. No. 13, Dean Road). He was succeeded by his sister Alice Boyd (14th laird) who never married but whom was a great friend of William Bell Scott, and other artists of the pre-Raphaelite school. The next to inherit was Margaret Courtney-Boyd (15th laird) and lastly, Evelyn May Courtney-Boyd (16th laird) who sold it to the highest bidder, Elton August Eckstrand an American from Grosse Point, Michigan. Eckstrand purchased it in 1978 in the pretext of making it an artist's haven. He named himself 18th laird* of Penkill and created the "Order of the Owl" (see the owl perched above the door in the photo) which was solely a venture to systematically loot the castle's treasures of art and furnishings over a 15 year period.

(continued page 2)

And You Thought Your House Was Old

The House of Boyd Society put this striking color photographic of the historic family castle on the front of their newsletter along with a story relating the castle's history. The rest of the newsletter is black and white, but the addition of color here makes it very eye-catching.

>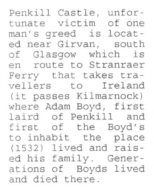
> "Many people have connected through the newsletter. It is fun when one finds that their neighbor is a relative."
> —**Richard G. Boyd**

Leetes from Around the World

The Leete Legacy is the newsletter for the Leete Family Association. The association has about 150 members and an overall membership list of 400 names. The association was founded in 1989 in conjunction with a Leete family reunion that coincided with the 350th anniversary of the founding of Guildford, CT. William Leete was one of the town founders and later a governor of Connecticut Colony.

The family association is open to anyone with an interest in the Leete family, not necessarily a family member. "Leete is an unusual family name, so most people bearing it are probably related—it's easier to trace than a common name like 'Cooper,'" says editor Cynthia Leet. "We have members in Great Britain, Australia, New Zealand and Canada."

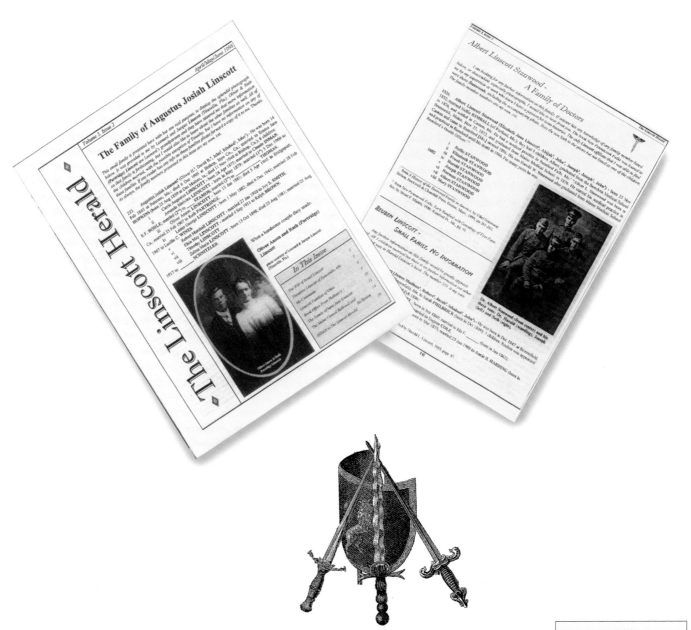

Family Stories Beget Family Stories

Jeff Linscott reports liking the contacts that the newsletter gives him with other family members. "Several cousins have 'found' each other as a result of printing stories about mutual grandparents or great-grandparents," says Jeff. "This results in more stories coming forth, which is the best reason for doing this in the first place."

❦ ❦ ❦

"In our family, as far as we are concerned, we were born and what happened before that is myth."

—V.S. Prichett,
British author

FOR BETTER OR FOR WORSE / By Lynn Johnston

IF YOU'RE SENDING A MESSAGE TO MICHAEL, LIZ-ASK HIM WHEN HE'S COMING HOME.

I DID.

AND?

HE'S NOT SURE. HE MIGHT STAY IN LONDON AND WORK ON A PROJECT WITH HIS ROOMMATE.

WHAT ABOUT HIS JOB AT MEGAFOOD?

I APPLIED FOR IT. HIS BOSS SAID HE'D TRY AN' GET ME ON DAY SHIFT.

WHY AM I ALWAYS THE LAST TO KNOW EVERYTHING?

YOU'RE NOT ON-LINE!

FOR BETTER OR FOR WORSE / By Lynn Johnston

MICHAEL AN' I SEND MESSAGES BACK AN' FORTH ALL THE TIME, MOM—AND WE GO INTO THESE CHATROOMS—SEE?

YOU MEAN YOU JUST TALK TO WHOEVER HAPPENS TO BE THERE?

SURE!

WHAT DO YOU TALK ABOUT?

HOMEWORK, MOVIES, PERSONAL STUFF... YOU JUST OPEN UP AN' SAY WHATEVER YOU WANNA SAY!

ISN'T IT DANGEROUS?

YEAH... MY WRISTS GET A LITTLE SORE SOMETIMES.

FOR BETTER OR FOR WORSE / By Lynn Johnston

HEY, UGLY BROTHER! WE WATCHED A BUNCH OF OLD SLIDES LAST NIGHT. IT WAS COOL!

REMEMBER WHEN YOU AND GORDON BLEW UP PINK RUBBER GLOVES AND ACTED LIKE COWS? REMEMBER THE SOCK-SNIFFING CONTEST?

THERE WERE SO MANY GREAT PICTURES OF YOU DOING THE DUMBEST THINGS!!!

HOW MUCH TO KEEP THEM OFF THE INTERNET?

CLICK TICK!

Chapter Six:
E-Mail and Web Site News

The most powerful impact of the Internet has been the creation of online "community." This becomes even more powerful when you start with a group, such as a family, that is already a community, and then draw them closer with technology.

The form that you publish in isn't an all or nothing thing. Many families send out their news in print form but also do what I call "cross publishing." By this I mean that they also publish additional news on a Web page, offer updates via e-mail or list family members' e-mail addresses so individuals can communicate directly online.

If you're thinking of electronic publishing, note that more people have access to e-mail than to the Internet. Even though e-mail messages are sent using the Internet connections, not everyone goes to Web pages every day. Most people connected to e-mail, however, do check their messages every day. So, let's start first with e-mail.

Sharing Letters with Everyone

When surveyed, most family newsletter editors say that their least favorite part of doing a printed newsletter is the production and the trip to the post office. Electronic newsletters bypass those steps and are delivered at no cost and instantly. Here are how some families are using e-mail.

❏ Submit articles for print newsletter.

❏ Submit articles for Web site.

❏ Send out birth announcements.

❏ List e-mail addresses for extended family members.

❏ Post e-mail addresses on family Web site calendars.

❏ Send international and friendship letters instantly.

❏ Add your news and pass it along in a chain letter.

❏ Broadcast letters to family address book.

> ❦ ❦ ❦
>
> "Since it is a plain fact that generations of our families no longer live in the same village, here at last is a new technology that provides an opportunity for all of us, everywhere, to connect and stay in touch, using one central location, one global 'refrigerator door'… that everyone in the family, no matter where they are in the world, can access at any time."
>
> —**Robin Williams**, writing in *Home Sweet Home Page* (see page 104)

> **Emoticons** are used in e-mails as a way to add humor and hugs. Turn your head to the left to see:
>
> :-) smiling
> :)   smiling
> :-D laughing
> ;-) winking
> :-o wow!
> 8-] wow, man
> :-| serious
> :-(frowning; sad
> :-[pouting
> :-@ screaming
> :-r sticking tongue out
> :-X   lips are sealed
> :( ) can't stop talking
> <:-| dunce
> : * kisses
> :-{} blowing a kiss
> O :-) angelic
> (::():) bandage

The advantage of e-mail over phone calls:

❑ Can time the reading and reply.

❑ More forgiving for different time zones.

❑ No awkward gaps in conversations.

❑ Some people are more expressive and give more details in writing (that's for you, Dad).

The advantage of e-mail over mail:

❑ More immediate.

❑ More predictable for international deliveries.

❑ Less expensive.

❑ More people will reply to your e-mail.

❑ Less of a clerical hassle.

Address Book

Edit Book   Select Address

Name   Address

Family

Delete   Edit... Group... Person...

Search Directories...

Address To   Files

Family

Now

SUBJECT
READ ME: The Blake Bulletin   Summer

MESSAGE
.... Blake Bulletin ....

News to Share from the Blake Family

READ ON FOR:

... Summer Reunion Time and Place Set
... Tim and Kristen's Vacation News
... Katie Graduates :)
... Rich and Beth's Big Surprise (read on to find out)
... Upcoming Events
... Submit Your News – Deadline for Next Issue

Send Later

SUMMER FAMILY REUNION SET
The Blake family reunion will be held on August 15 at the Springfield City Park
main pavilion. The event will start at noon and will last until dark. Several
members of the extended family have RSVP'd that they'll attend; even Steven is
getting a leave to come home from Germany for the reunion.

Format

Spelling

☐ Return Receipts Requested From AOL Members

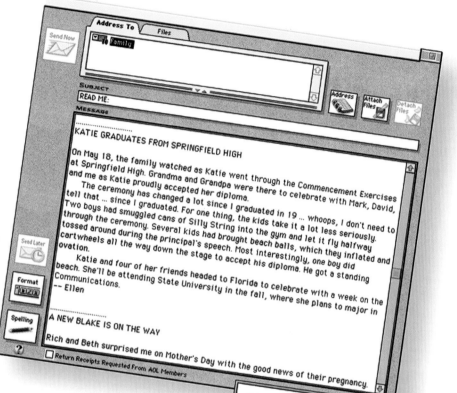

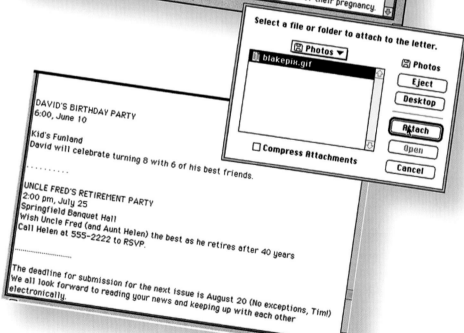

Publish the e-mail addresses of family in the print newsletter. Allows you to start your database of e-mail addresses and then, eventually, go to an e-mail newsletter. The e-mail newsletter can have links (if you use Eudora) to photos published on the Web site.

Online and On Time
This e-mail newsletter comes out seasonally. It evolved from an annual print newsletter. Family members are now more prompt with their submissions since they can write and send their news without leaving their desks.

Netscape: frameset.htm

Location:

Gallery 1
Gallery 2
Max says...
Potpourri
Kiddles!
Links
M&J

MAIL

He likes to show off!

Max says...

```
"baba".........bottle
"wawa".........water
"ttth".........kathy
"wow"..........wow
"ahdun".........all done
"keech".........cheese
"lefsuh".......lefse
"oost".........toast
"byebye".........I bid you a safe journey
"yeow".........kitten
```

Murray Goes Multi-Media

This Web site shows the value of "cross-publishing." Murray publishes a black and white text-only printed newsletter that lists the Web site and invites readers to join him online. On the site, readers get to see these cute color photos of son Max. He also lists his e-mail address in print and links to it on his Web site to encourage electronic responses.

❦ ❦ ❦

"Over the 19 years that I've been doing a family newsletter, the format has changed with changing technology. I started with hand lettering and black and white photocopying and have gone to computer-aided drawing and color printing. Moving to the Web was a natural progression."

—**Nancy**

Hidden Treasure for Family & Friends

Nancy maintains a Web site for her speaking and writing business but she includes a special link for family and friends. She tells them to click on the eye of the figure on her site to jump to a photo scrapbook.

Families spread throughout the world can stay involved with each other's lives online. This family site includes photos, news, stories, genealogical information, birthdays and anniversaries and even the family cookbook. The calendar listings include links that connect directly to the person's e-mail, making it easy to check the calendar and send a quick message of congratulations or best wishes.

Location: http://www.c...nclan.com/genealogy/index.htm

| What's New | What's Cool | Destinations | Net Search | People | Software |

Our Family Tree

Welcome to our C....n Family Tree! Here you will find genealogical information about our patriarchs and their descendents. Our heritage is very important to us as an extended family, and we hope you find our efforts to share our past with you both educational and entertaining.

Table of Contents

Our Family Tree

Surname List

Index of Names

Back to Main Page

| What's New | What's Cool | Destinations | Net Search | People | Software |

La Unión

The Family Newsletter -- Vol. 6, No. 1   February

Michelle Weds Carlos in New York

We received this lovely e-mail from Susu the day of Michellita's wedding. She wanted to make sure that we absorbed every detail. Thank you, Susu, (sorry, I can't seem to change that in my mind!); thank you for writing everything while it was fresh in your mind. We did feel as if we were there!

Date: 12/13/97

Today was a beautiful sunny day. It was cold but not too cold. A perfect day for a wedding. Believe it or not, Michelle was to get married today. What a day to rejoice! The church was a beautiful small church, all decked out for Advent, beautiful stained glass windows, a gorgeous center aisle decorated with white billowy bows. It was a great day for reunions. Mikie and his new bride Maria were there. Eddie and Linda, Teresa, Stevie (looking GREAT! Thank GOD!) and Denise, Momi and Eddie were all waiting patiently.

Of course, all the López' were

Our Family Profiles | Family Newsletters | Family Cookbook | Birthdays & Anniversaries
Family Photo Albums | Family Fund Summary | Family Tree | Family Internet Address Book | Links
Download Excite PAL | Download Netscape Communicator | Sign our guestbook | View our guestbook
Top of page

01554
Visitors since July 1, 1997

E-mail our webmaster with your comments.   Copyright © 1997-1998,   and family
Last updated: May 02, 1998   All rights reserved

❦ ❦ ❦

"Mom said I was born with a question mark in my mouth. I enjoy the queries and the hunt for answers. I run every name in queries through my indices for all past issues and come up with a lot of answers. I have been able to tie about 35 people together who are chasing the same ancestors, however, I have not been able to connect to my own past ca 1800. Most keep kidding me that when I find mine I'll quit publishing Havens Harbor. Not so. I find looking for theirs more fun—I'm tired of looking for mine!"

—Jo Havens

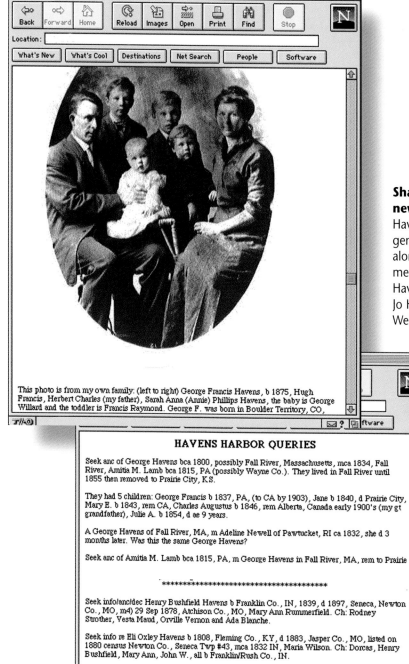

This photo is from my own family: (left to right) George Francis Havens, b 1875, Hugh Francis, Herbert Charles (my father), Sarah Anna (Annie) Phillips Havens, the baby is George Willard and the toddler is Francis Raymond. George F. was born in Boulder Territory, CO,

HAVENS HARBOR QUERIES

Seek anc of George Havens bca 1800, possibly Fall River, Massachusetts, mca 1834, Fall River, Amitia M. Lamb bca 1815, PA (possibly Wayne Co.). They lived in Fall River until 1855 then removed to Prairie City, KS.

They had 5 children: George Francis b 1837, PA, (to CA by 1903), Jane b 1840, d Prairie City, Mary E. b 1843, rem CA, Charles Augustus b 1846, rem Alberta, Canada early 1900's (my gt grandfather), Julie A. b 1854, d ae 9 years.

A George Havens of Fall River, MA, m Adeline Newell of Pawtucket, RI ca 1832, she d 3 months later. Was this the same George Havens?

Seek anc of Amitia M. Lamb bca 1815, PA, m George Havens in Fall River, MA, rem to Prairie

****

Seek info/anc/dec Henry Bushfield Havens b Franklin Co., IN, 1839, d 1897, Seneca, Newton Co., MO, m4) 29 Sep 1878, Atchison Co., MO, Mary Ann Rummerfield. Ch: Rodney Strother, Vesta Maud, Orville Vernon and Ada Blanche.

Seek info re Eli Oxley Havens b 1808, Fleming Co., KY, d 1883, Jasper Co., MO, listed on 1880 census Newton Co., Seneca Twp #43, mca 1832 IN, Maria Wilson. Ch: Dorcas, Henry Bushfield, Mary Ann, John W., all b Franklin/Rush Co., IN.

Seek info/anc/dec Orrel Vernon Havens, age 7 on 07 Jan 1928, sister Irene Esher, age 10, 09 Dec 1928? POB MO?

Answer: I can get you back to John1, John2, John3, Eli O.4, Henry Bushfield5. The info is in HH3:3 (53), HH4:1 (62), HH5:2 (99), HH5:3 and HH5:4, HH6:1 has corrections to BR 19. The #'s in parens are BR #'s that were incorporated into BR 19 after they connected.

HH5:2 & HH5:4 answer your Henry Bushfield and Orrel Vernon queries. The others are tie ins to this Branch 19 line. I have back issues for $8.00 each, or if you get 4 or more, they are $7.00 each.

Sharing the old with new technology. The Havens family shares genealogical queries along with photos and memorabilia on the Havens Harbor section of Jo Havens's commercial Web site.

Family and School Uses of the Internet

The following are some of the ways people are using the Internet:

❑ Using chat rooms to "talk" online.

❑ Sharing genealogical information of family Web sites.

❑ Individuals and nuclear family Web pages.

❑ Posting school pages online—getting kids involved in doing their own school newspaper online.

❑ Posting photos and scrapbooks on Web pages.

❑ Sending e-mail news.

❑ Listing reunion news on a Web site.

❑ E-mailing reunion reminders.

❑ Holding virtual events online—family members can see birthdays or participate in a reunion from their computer screen.

Finding Family Online

To see if your extended family has a genealogical site on line, use these tips for using the search engines to find it.

❑ If you have an unusual last name, entering it into a search engine should be enough to get you started — it should at least bring up some personal home pages of people with your last name.

❑ If you have a common last name and you know what region of the country your family is from, enter your name in quotation marks along with the region in quotation marks and plus signs in front of both, i.e. +"Smith" +"Kentucky."

❑ Try your family name plus the word newsletter, i.e. +"Smith" +"newsletter."

❑ Enter your family name plus the word family or association, i.e. +"Smith" +"association."

❑ Search by your family name plus the word genealogy, i.e. +"Smith" +"genealogy."

❑ Some genealogy sites include searchable databases. Go to one of the genealogy sites listed in the Publishing Tools section and look for your family name.

❑ If your last name (like mine) is also a first name, try putting it with the word family in quotation marks or adding the word surname, i.e. "Floyd family" or +"Floyd" +"surname."

A Note About Privacy

Accessibility is both a benefit and a drawback of the Internet. Because most sites are available to anyone who is online, avoid putting any sensitive information such as addresses and phone numbers. Even if you don't register with the search engines, some search engines will eventually find your site, or your site can be added by someone else. Instead, check with your Internet Service Provider about setting up a password-protected site.

> ❦ ❦ ❦
>
> "The Web site has been a big help in getting the word out. I have gotten a lot of information from people who come across the Web page and just drop me a line to say I have a connection to the Demuth family."
>
> **—Patrick Demuth**

> ❦ ❦ ❦
>
> "You hear a lot of dialogue on the death of the American family. Families aren't dying. They're merging into big conglomerates."
>
> **—Erma Bombeck**

18 Months

with

Alexandre Maxime Peter

June '92 to Dec. '93

September '92

Freedom. Finally got out of that bassinet. Sure, it was cute at first but so's a studio apartment. My mother was delighted that I could now roll over. (Lady, I could do it before but just didn't have the real estate.)

My parents seem a bit wiped out from the move. I wanted to stick around longer for the rest of Hurricane Andrew. I miss all the fun.

The great discussion around this place has been the date of my first smile. They can't yet distinguish *joy* from *gas*. According to Amy Vanderbilt, it isn't proper for me to confess.

They Grow So Fast...

The first eighteen months of my son's life, I was a disorganized wreck except for two things—I wrote in my journal almost every day and took photographs like a fiend. Once I had a moment to collect my thoughts, I put them into a book to share with my family and to keep for my son.

Chapter Seven:
The Idea Gallery

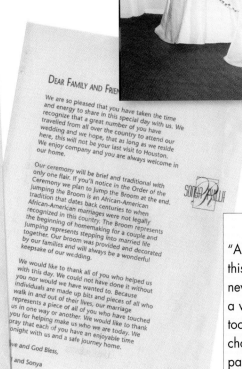

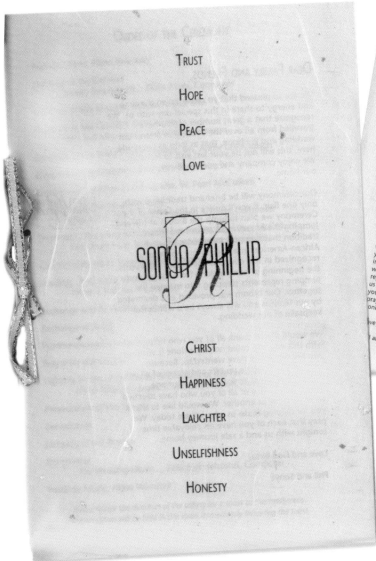

TRUST

HOPE

PEACE

LOVE

SONYA PHILLIP

CHRIST

HAPPINESS

LAUGHTER

UNSELFISHNESS

HONESTY

DEAR FAMILY AND FRIEN

We are so pleased that you have taken the time and energy to share in this special day with us. We recognize that a great number of you have travelled from all over the country to attend our wedding and we hope, that as long as we reside here, this will not be your last visit to Houston. We enjoy company and you are always welcome in our home.

Our ceremony will be brief and traditional with only one flair. If you'll notice in the Order of the Ceremony we plan to Jump the Broom at the end. Jumping the Broom is an African-American tradition that dates back centuries to when African-American marriages were not legally recognized in this country. The Broom represents the beginning of homemaking for a couple and Jumping represents stepping into married life together. Our broom was provided and decorated by our families and will always be a wonderful keepsake of our wedding.

We would like to thank all of you who helped us with this day. We could not have done it without you nor would we have wanted to. Because individuals are made up bits and pieces of all who walk in and out of their lives, our marriage represents a piece of all of you who have touched us in one way or another. We would like to thank you for helping make us who we are today. We pray that each of you have an enjoyable time onight with us and a safe journey home.

ve and God Bless,

l and Sonya

SONYA PHILLIP

❧ ❧ ❧

"A dear friend made this program and newsletter for me as a wedding gift. She took great care in choosing just the right paper. Another friend's mother got misty eyed when she first saw it at the ceremony—she said that it reminded her so much of me."

—Sonya

Something New

Sonya and Phillip's wedding newsletter is both elegant and warm with its moving message to family and friends and rich paper colors and texture. The letter from the couple talks about bringing old traditions into the present as they prepare to start their new life together.

Cousin Naomi Joki laid to rest in Bonney Cemetery

Here follows part of the words spoken at the gravesite by her brother Jesse Bonney:

Our family has come today to bring to its final resting place the mortal remains of Naomi Bonney Joki. Husband Bob could not be with us. However, he specifically requested that what we do here today include the playing of the bagpipes.

Naomi Hope Bonney was born to her parents Clarence and Edith Bonney on February 7, 1924, in Mitchell, South Dakota. She suffered a heart attack and died after a short hospital stay on September 27, 1997 in Tacoma at the age of 73.

Naomi was a daughter of South Dakota: its fields and pastures; its sun, its wind, its rain, its heat and its cold; its blizzards, its grasshoppers and its drought; its prosperity and its depression; but more importantly she was a daughter of its culture, its heritage and its values...transmitted down from pioneer grandparents through her parents, and little changed in the passage.

But most importantly, however, Naomi caught something of the spirit of the Pearl Creek Church. In what turned out to be her last words to the family, she affirmed to me her faith in Jesus. I asked if she was trusting in Jesus. Her eyes opened wide and she replied, "Yes." We never spoke again.

Her early years were spent in the farm home of her parents located a half mile south of where we stand today. She received her elementary school education in the Rhoads school a half mile north of here. During those early years she faithfully attended church and Sunday School in the Pearl Creek Methodist Church just over into Beadle County.

She attended Forestburg High School, Wessington Springs College, Seattle Pacific College, University of Washington, receiving a Master of Social Work degree in 1962.

In grade 7 she decided to teach, so she started her professional career with four years of teaching at Wessington Springs High School.

She then worked for the State of Washington Department of Public Assistantce as caseworker and supervisor of caseworkers. Then she was a psychiatric social worker at the U. of W. Hospital in the Child Psychiatry Out-Patient Clinic, then a school social worker for Tacoma Public Schools.

Concurrent with her professional career of helping others, she found time to be a homemaker and particularly to mother her stepchildren.

And so we meet today at this cemetery near her childhood home. It is fitting that she chose this spot as her final resting place.

This land was given for a cemetery by her grandfather, George H. Bonney.

Many of her relatives lie here. Her great grandfather Bonney, her grandparents Bonney, her father and mother Bonney, a baby sister, Doris May, who died at birth, two uncles, an aunt (Roger Bonney, Wilma and Les Thomas) and many friends and neighbors from her early years all are buried here.

And so we have come to lay to rest our sister, our mother, our auntie, our cousin, our friend. Farewell sister. We will see you over There in The Morning.

Grave sites in the Bonney Cemetery are free to all Bonneys interested. Contact Sexton Warren Thomas

Letter from the "first grandchild"

At the Black Hills reunion, senior cousins were asked to recall memories of their grandparents. The memories were recorded on video by Bob Pattison, husband of Polly.

Between reunions he edited the conversations and interspersed them with memorable moments of reunion activities. The video was shown at the Colorado reunion. If you missed seeing it, ask the senior cousins from your clan who attended to show it to you.

One memory that could not be recorded on that video comes from the person our grandparents called "Their first grandchild" (or so they put in her baby book.)

Eleanore Rowan Moe, whose mother was Aunt Wilma's best friend, hoped to join us in Colorado to show us her baby book and tell us more stories of our grandparents. She couldn't make it, so sent this by letter to Carol Ann Francis instead:

"I have many wonderful memories of what seemed a huge home to me, with that big front porch where Grandpa Bonney greeted us from his rocking chair. My favorite memory of him was sitting on his lap in the rocking chair, hearing his stories. My favorite story was when he told how they twisted hay for fuel for the potbellied stove. He made all kinds of motions to show me the exact method to generate the most heat.

"Your Grandpa Bonney was a very

well-educated man, (perhaps self-educated?) who was highly respected wherever he went. We went to the Old Settlers' picnics which were in the Bonney grove. Food was in abundance. In those days, the women took great pride in producing one of their favorite recipes. The music and most of the program was from the Bonney clan.

"Grandpa Bonney always gave a speech and **everyone** listened. It was usually a patriotic speech, but he always brought God into it, so it was sort of a sermon. He lived his religion. Pearl Creek Church meant SO much to him. All of you come from very fine stock.

"I shall never forget the morning that the old house burned. I was staying with your family (during my first year of university in Minneapolis.) We were all seated at the breakfast table when the phone rang. Your mother went into the kitchen to answer it. She returned and in a calm voice said, "The old home place just burned this morning." Evidently she did not want to disturb you children as she must have been terribly emotional inside.

"Have a wonderful reunion and maybe I can join you next time."

Eleanore would love to meet any Bonneys, and tell more of her stories of the olden days.

Sharing and Keeping Family Memories in Times of Grief

Funerals draw together family and friends in a way that's similar to reunions but more emotional. Often this emotion leads to an outpouring of family stories and reminiscences. These can be recorded to share with family and friends who are unable to attend as well as to save. Use a newsletter to:

❑ Share stories told by friends and family.

❑ List the songs, Bible verses, poems and other readings from the funeral.

❑ Create a timeline of the person's life.

❑ List typical expressions they used and things they loved.

❑ Save the memorial write-up along with the obituary and guest book in the family archives.

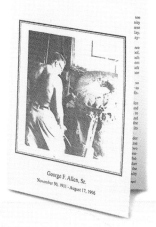

George F. Allen, Sr.
November 30, 1911 - August 17, 1996

Front

A Son's Tribute

My earliest memories are clear
Of a hard working foundryman
The father who was always near.

He taught me an honorable trade
Insisting I work as other men,
Of dirt and sweat to be unafraid.

I've seen him laugh and fight and lead,
And work when lesser men would drop.
Few other examples did I ever need.

Yes Dad, this is a tribute to You.
For all that you have meant and mean to me.
From a son who rarely told you so
I love you.

GFA, Jr.

Big George

'I wish I had but didn't, and now I'm sorry I can't!' Too frequent, too late, words of many sons and daughters reflecting on the lost opportunity to pay tribute to a parent or loved one. Such was the motivation when these words were first penned ten years ago on the occasion of Dad's birthday. But then, the following paragraphs could have easily been written by anyone who knew Big George.

The foundry is long gone and now so is the foundryman. But to three generations of Sewell children attending the neighboring elementary school, Dad was always Mister Allen. They and their teachers looked forward each year to visiting his aluminum and brass foundry. It was a mystery to them how their brass paperweight mementos were formed from the large black dirt piles they saw there. For many students, this was their first experience seeing men hard at work earning a living.

For many years he was known as Big George around Sewell. Not so much for his size, though he was always a barrel of a man, but simply to differentiate him from his eldest son, little George. Big George was a fitting nickname for other reasons as well.

Remember the tornado that tore through Sewell in the late 1950s? Fallen trees blocked Mantua Blvd. and Center Street. Power lines were down and a few buildings destroyed. Who motivated and organized Sewell men to cut and move the trees and cleanup after the disaster? Big George. And where did many town women cook that evening? In the foundry, using the big propane - fired core baking oven. Every town has a paladin during its time of need and Sewell had Big George.

Dad not only excelled as family head, businessman and courageous leader but shouldered civic and spiritual responsibilities as well. As a longtime Boy Scout leader, he influenced many Sewell boys. He saw his own two sons achieve scouting's highest rank, become Marine officers and responsible business and family men in their own right. His daughter Nancy, followed her Dad's example as a servant - leader. She became a homemaker and serves her community as a teacher. And Big George is probably the only Cedarville Methodist to become a deacon at the Sewell Community Baptist Church.

(continued next page)

Then there's the stuff of which memories and legends are made. Fresh Jersey clams steaming on a cherry red furnace lid at the end of a long, grimy workday at the foundry. A big tin of melted butter and gallon of unsweetened iced tea stand nearby to make for a South Jersey delicacy and fixin's without equal. Big George and his workmen standing around the furnace swapping tales. I still savor the scene more than thirty years later.

How 'bout running your hand quickly and smoothly through a six inch long stream of molten aluminum flowing from a smoking crucible into a sand mold - without being severely burned. Or just flicking your finger through the molten stream as I was inclined to do, surprised at the mildly warm sensation of the liquid metal. Strange it was then and strange today.

An old foundryman's secret, I was told.

Now I hardly remember this, but boyhood legend has it that old-fashioned bare knuckle boxing matches were held in the cornfield out back of the foundry. The friendly but serious combatants were Big George and one or another of his employees. That has something to do with Dad's earlier days as an amateur boxer at the Camden YMCA.

One scene I do remember - clearly, is an incident involving a family pet, a large Collie accidentally pinned under the car. As the vehicle was being jacked up to free Gay, Big George slid under the car and encouraged the big dog to fasten its large jaws firmly on his muscular forearm. The dog bit down firmly, hard enough to bear his pain, but not enough to break Dad's skin. Big George in turn, quietly bore the dog's pain until it was freed. An unforgettable example of his willingness to share another's burden. This was the same dog that years earlier saved Mark's life by racing across the yard, leaping and snaring a large crazed rat just as it attacked.

Dad never was one to give much advice, write letters, or try to impress. But I well remember her Mother. And there was the single handwritten note he sent me while I was in Vietnam. It was one of the most treasured I received during the year I was there. And impress? He didn't have to try.

His example at home and at work was all his kids and those that knew him, ever needed.

Back

Celebrating the Life of the Foundryman

This memorial card includes a poem, "A Son's Tribute," from George, Jr., that he wrote to his father while he was still living. The card itself was prepared after the death of George, Sr., and included the poem along with the reminder of the importance of honoring family members while they're still living.

To keep your place when interrupted by life's everyday catastrophes*

The Official
Taylor Charles Hunt
Baby Bookmark

Uh-oh, looks like one of those emergencies. Gotta Go!

*This list includes wet diapers, not enough food, ringing phones, too much food, business meetings, cold baths, not enough sleep, bright lights, too much sleep, not enough kisses, boring books.

"We traveled to Canada for my brother's wedding when Taylor was just a few weeks old. The hospital hadn't yet sent Taylor's birth certificate and the airline official wasn't going to let us take the baby out of the U.S. without it. All I had with me was this bookmark that I'd made as a birth announcement. I showed it to the official and he let us through."

—Richard

Spring 1994
New Titles
Selected Backlist

Hot off the Presses

Proud father Richard creates book-oriented birth announcements for each of his children. He created the bookmark (shown to the left) for his son Taylor.

Above was a more ambitious project for Rachel in which he gives her rave "reviews." Richard—he's in the publishing business, as you can guess—uses terms from the book industry, such as "new release" and "stand alone volume" in writing about little Rachel and even includes an article written from Rachel's point of view in which she gets to comment on her new surroundings.

Richard and Linda's third child is due any day…will he get his own CD-ROM?

Rachel Helene Hunt

A WORK IN PROGRESS
NOVEL, in every way, POETIC, sure,
NON-FICTION, too, let's call it
MULTI-MEDIA

A brand new collection of chromosomes, gurgles,
quirks, and craziness, created by the same folks
responsible for big brother Taylor.[1] While it's possible to consider these two works as companion
volumes or bookends of a sort, this newest edition
is most definitely <u>not</u> simply a sequel, but instead a
joyfully illuminating different creation, bringing
together an original new voice and unique perspective in this stand-alone volume (although we live in
fear of the day when "stand-alone" literally happens; the idea of both of them mobile is a very
scary thought).

Exquisitely packaged, this slim volume carries the
highest production values available today. With
design accents of pink and white throughout, the
hand-sewn bindings fit nice and snug, keeping her
warm and happy.

> Publication Date: June 6, 1994 at 2:55 p.m.
> Shipping weight: 6 lbs, 6 oz.
> Spine: Flexi-bound
> Trim size: 19 3/4"
> SS # - t.k.
> Multi-media
> Simultaneous release on Audio

---
[1] Amount of responsibility depends on physical proximity, decibel level
and total amount of comprehensive insurance if he did something really
wicked.

An excerpt from Rachel's early work:

So this is being born. The trick is, of course, figuring out how to deal
with everything, all at once. Like the enormous faces that occasionally hover
above me. What does one say to to a head that's bigger than my entire body?
How does one maintain composure when staring back at an eye twice the size of
my foot, a situation which gives a fresh slant on both Kafka and all those old
biology slides of the compound eyes of a fruit fly.

I guess it's true what my Dad's always thinking, that you have to put
yourself in the other person's place before you can understand how they feel.
Oh, by the way, that's one of the coolest things about being a newborn...being
able to hear what everyone, and everything, is thinking. This includes the stray
thoughts and lonely musings of what most grown-ups consider inanimate
objects: the phone, the rug, the cat, stuffed animals. Remember this the next time
you plop yourself down on the couch. Now you know why so many babies
assume that stunned look when a group of adults crowd around—the cacophony
of a dozen conversations all at once, booming inside and out, from folks who
loom as large as a block of four story buildings. It's the Tower of Babel, tenfold.
Alice in Wonderland run amuck. Thankfully, Taylor, my brother, can still talk to
me without smacking lips, which is what we newborns call talking, so he fills me
in as to the origin and purpose a lot of the strange stuff that happens out here.

But to be honest, nothing yet has warranted any extraordinary reaction or inspired any lyricism on my part. I think even Amy Vanderbilt would be
stumped when trying to come up with an appropriate response to "She's just a
little bird," or "She looks like a gnome," or worst of all, any comparisons to
raisins, peanuts, apple dumplings, sugar-puffs or any other food stuff that's
small, sweet or wrinkly. Also, at this point, I believe that "precious" should be
struck from the English language. So basically I'm waiting them out, figuring that
if I don't respond to all the saccharine stuff, maybe they'll move on to some
more engaging subjects soon.

Idle conversations aside, living outside the womb is a magnificent
experience: the colors, the sounds, the smells (oops, except mine), music, laughter, all the impassioned exhortations of mankind engaged in this thing called life.
Personally, I'm thrilled because now that I'm out I just holler if I need something. Before, I could yell all I want, but nobody ever heard or paid any attention
until I kicked somebody (sorry Mom).

Woman of the Nineties, you bet. Thanks to Nancy Friday, Helen
Gurley Brown, Naomi Wolf, Betty Friedan and Susan Faludi, all the early suffrag-
ists, and anyone else who has broken ground in the long struggle for women's
rights. Let's ride, cowgirl

Every day as parents, we learn more about the pure magic of life.
Big events like Rachel's birth obviously transcend the day-to-day and
force us to seek a vantage point from which to see beyond the horizon,
trying our best to anticipate what our children will confront during their
lifetimes. This long-distance focus is not an exclusive or priviliged view,
but too often gets lost in the crush of deadlines and daily crises.
This said, we remind ourselves to live by two Native American sayings,
in an attempt to makes this world a better place: 1. This earth is
not ours, we are only borrowing it from our children, and, 2.
In our every deliberation, we must consider the impact of our decisions
upon the next seven generations.

Spring 1994
New Titles
Selected Backlist

> ❦ ❦ ❦
>
> "One year, when money was tight, I tried to cut back my 300-name mailing list. I received tons of calls and mail from those who missed their letter. They all asked what had happened. So many people told me that they saved them and really loved seeing the kids growing."
>
> **—Nancy**

Since part of Nancy's business is creating Mindscapes (mapping business situations, teams and plans), she shares this special talent in her holiday newsletter for family and friends. She either sketches the pictures or pastes on parts of photos to her original map. Then, she takes it to a color photocopy service for duplication.

Your mindmap newsletter could be with words instead of graphics. Use the technique for clustering shown on page 34.

Create a Mindscape or Mindmap Newsletter

❑ **Leave room to add a special note.** Nancy uses the same color pen to write the personalized notes that she uses to draw the newsletter. She fills in the thought "bubbles" above the photos with different messages.

❑ **Create a picture/thought bubble version**. Using the idea above, your newsletter could be a mixture of photos from your family with "fill in the bubbles" above each photo. The heading for the newsletter could be "you're in our thoughts."

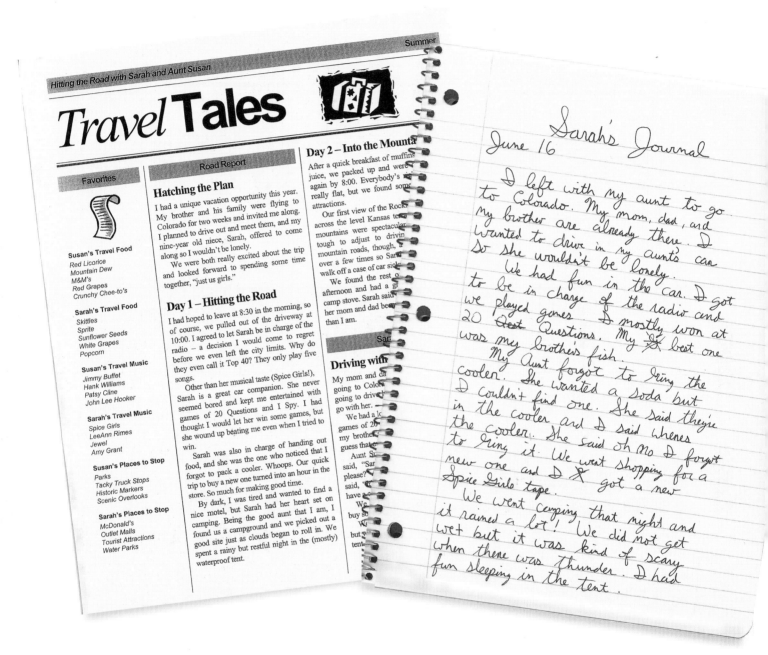

Summer

Hitting the Road with Sarah and Aunt Susan

Travel Tales

Favorites

Susan's Travel Food
Red Licorice
Mountain Dew
M&M's
Red Grapes
Crunchy Chee-to's

Sarah's Travel Food
Skittles
Sprite
Sunflower Seeds
White Grapes
Popcorn

Susan's Travel Music
Jimmy Buffet
Hank Williams
Patsy Cline
John Lee Hooker

Sarah's Travel Music
Spice Girls
LeeAnn Rimes
Jewel
Amy Grant

Susan's Places to Stop
Parks
Tacky Truck Stops
Historic Markers
Scenic Overlooks

Sarah's Places to Stop
McDonald's
Outlet Malls
Tourist Attractions
Water Parks

Road Report

Hatching the Plan

I had a unique vacation opportunity this year. My brother and his family were flying to Colorado for two weeks and invited me along. I planned to drive out and meet them, and my nine-year old niece, Sarah, offered to come along so I wouldn't be lonely.

We were both really excited about the trip and looked forward to spending some time together, "just us girls."

Day 1 – Hitting the Road

I had hoped to leave at 8:30 in the morning, so of course, we pulled out of the driveway at 10:00. I agreed to let Sarah be in charge of the radio – a decision I would come to regret before we even left the city limits. Why do they even call it Top 40? They only play five songs.

Other than her musical taste (Spice Girls!), Sarah is a great car companion. She never seemed bored and kept me entertained with games of 20 Questions and I Spy. I had thought I would let her win some games, but she wound up beating me even when I tried to win.

Sarah was also in charge of handing out food, and she was the one who noticed that I forgot to pack a cooler. Whoops. Our quick trip to buy a new one turned into an hour in the store. So much for making good time.

By dark, I was tired and wanted to find a nice motel, but Sarah had her heart set on camping. Being the good aunt that I am, I found us a campground and we picked out a good site just as clouds began to roll in. We spent a rainy but restful night in the (mostly) waterproof tent.

Day 2 – Into the Mountains

After a quick breakfast of muffins juice, we packed up and were again by 8:00. Everybody's really flat, but we found some attractions.

Our first view of the Rock across the level Kansas te mountains were spectacular tough to adjust to drivin mountain roads, though, a over a few times so Sara walk off a case of car sick

We found the rest afternoon and had a g camp stove. Sarah said her mom and dad be than I am.

Sar

Driving with

My mom and da going to Colo going to driv go with her.

We had a l games of 20 my brothe guess thate

Aunt Su said, "Sar please?" said, " have

We buy s W but tent

June 16   Sarah's Journal

I left with my aunt to go to Colorado. My mom, dad, and my brother are already there. I wanted to drive in my aunt's car so she wouldn't be lonely.

We had fun in the car. I got to be in charge of the radio and we played games. I mostly won at 20 Best Questions. My best one was my brother's fish.

My Aunt forgot to bring the cooler. She wanted a soda but I couldn't find one. She said they're in the cooler and I said whenes the cooler. She said oh no I forgot to bring it. We went shopping for a new one and I got a new Spice Girls tape.

We went camping that night and it rained a lot! We did not get wet but it was kind of scary when there was thunder. I had fun sleeping in the tent.

Quick and Easy Vacation Newsletter

Keeping a vacation journal captures stories that can be used in a newsletter and also gives you a record of the trip that can be reread and enjoyed years later. Having kids keep journals helps them remember what's special about a vacation and also lets you see the trip through their eyes. This newsletter was created using a word processor and one of the templates from *Quick and Easy Newsletters* (see Publishing Tools on page 104).

NewsTools Index

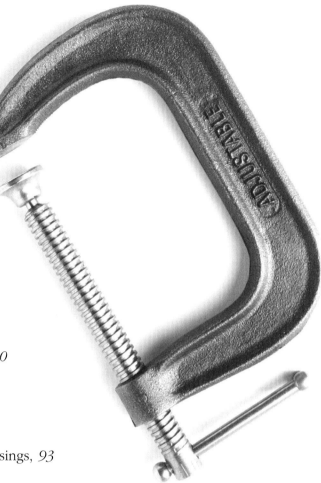

NewsTools:
Idea Tools

Ideas for What to Write About

Stuck? Here are hundreds of ways to avoid the blank page (or blinking cursor) syndrome. Get your pen handy and check the items that you want to include in your newsletter. As you go through the list, take a glance at the sample news items along the way.

Family News *(for individual families or extended families)*

Home

❑ Update on home renovations
❑ Update on new landscaping
❑ News of move
❑ Fun stories from move
❑ Retirement relocations
❑ News of building a new house
❑ Notes to neighbors
❑ Details of guest accommodations
❑ Fun things to do nearby
❑ Invitations to friends and family to visit
❑ Directions to house
❑ New address

Children

❑ Baptisms
❑ Christenings
❑ First communions
❑ Graduations
❑ How tall the kids are; how much they weigh
❑ Babies due
❑ Contests won

❦ ❦ ❦

"I start this news extravaganza with the announcement of a new addition to our family. A 10 pound 5 ounce baby girl named Sparkle. Tammie and I argued over a name and couldn't come to an agreement. So, since Patrick did such a nice job in picking Sara's name, we let him pick the dog's name. Yeah, I said dog! You think I would name a baby 'Sparkle'? Spark is a 3 month old black Labrador mix we picked up from the Humane Society. So far, she has been a great dog. She will be an even better dog when we get her house broken."

—Sean

- ❏ New hobbies
- ❏ Fun things that children say
- ❏ Reports from college students
- ❏ Kids corner
- ❏ School updates
- ❏ Sports updates
- ❏ Fun stories
- ❏ Accomplishments (learning to read, tie shoes, learning to drive)

Relationships

- ❏ Renewed wedding vows
- ❏ News of marriages
- ❏ Announcements of engagements

Friendships

- ❏ Friends who've visited
- ❏ Things that haven't changed about you or your friends
- ❏ Notes of thanks

Sports and hobbies

- ❏ Alma mater sports news (if sent to college friends)
- ❏ Sports you're still playing
- ❏ Hobbies you're still doing
- ❏ New sports and hobbies
- ❏ Places you traveled to for sports or hobbies

Pets

- ❏ New additions
- ❏ Old favorites
- ❏ Unusual pets and critters
- ❏ What kind
- ❏ Bad habits
- ❏ Interesting tricks
- ❏ Fun pet stories

Jobs

- ❏ Accomplishments
- ❏ Interesting business trips taken
- ❏ Favorite parts
- ❏ Any frustrations (doublecheck your mailing list first)
- ❏ Jobs lost
- ❏ Going back to school
- ❏ Classes taken just for fun
- ❏ Retirement plans
- ❏ Sideline business

> ❧ ❧ ❧
>
> "Our house has gone through tremendous change. We found severe termite damage when removing walls and parts of the floor and ended up tearing down all of the house except for the front porch. It was very sad seeing our house torn down, but led to new possibilities of design. Tim designed the replacement keeping the old charm but adding features (like a fireplace, Jacuzzi tub, and upstairs laundry room and a central vacuum system) that will make us comfortable for years to come. The girls are excited to each have her own room, and I am excited to have a walk-in closet. We moved out of our house to make it larger, into a rental house that was smaller. This has been a real challenge and has made me less of a clutter bug, but not much. Smiles."
>
> **—Charlotte**

Life changes

❑ Adjusting to changes (move, job, baby)

❑ Plans for coming year

❑ Things you're looking forward to

Vacations

❑ Where did you go?

❑ Why did you choose this destination?

❑ What special things happened while you were on vacation?

❑ Ask each family member for his or her favorite memory from the trip.

❑ Make a list of sights, sounds, smells and tastes from the trip.

❑ Write your vacation stories as a "how to" (or "how not to"). For example, write "How to keep four kids entertained on a ten hour car trip" or "How to avoid divorce on an extended camping trip."

❑ What did you like best about the place you visited (weather, food, scenery, etc.)?

❑ What surprised you that you didn't expect about the place you visited?

Timelines

❑ Special events from each month or season

❑ Scrapbook of family photos from the past year with captions

❑ Lists for each family member of newsworthy events in work or school, hobbies, sports, family life, relationships

Top 10 lists (Top 3, Top 5, etc.)

❑ Children's coined words or mispronunciations

❑ Phrases you (as parents) overuse

❑ Things you're most proud of

❑ Things you're most thankful for

❑ Happiest family moments

❑ Things you're looking forward to for next year

❑ Changes over the past year

❑ Books you've read

❑ Favorite movies of the year

❑ Favorite places

❑ Favorite songs of the year

Theme issues

Give your newsletter a theme, such as "change," "firsts," or "chaos" and tie all your stories into that theme.

❦ ❦ ❦

"We couldn't have made a change like this without the help of family and friends, especially:

• Chris and Shelly who threw us a party to kick us out of town, and welcomed us home during the Thanksgiving holidays.

• Aunt Joy and her family who welcomed us into her home with lots of love as we waited for our house to be completed.

• Brian and April who babysat for us during their family vacation while we were moving into our new house. Your timing was impeccable.

• To our new neighbors in Florida who have welcomed us in the community with open arms. We were lucky to pick a neighborhood with such wonderful families.

And finally to our families, whose understanding and support were unbending."

—Sean

Extended Family News

Use in addition to the items listed previously as well as with items listed under "Reunion" and "Genealogy."

❏ Poems (Mother's Day, Father's Day, memorials)
❏ Health update listing those with illnesses
❏ Prayer list
❏ Family tree updates
❏ Family mission statements (see Steven Covey's *The 7 Habits of Highly Effective Families,* listed on page 104)
❏ Requests for donations
❏ News by geographical area
❏ Genealogy books available on your family
❏ Letter from editor
❏ Opinions and editorials
❏ Family historic dates
❏ Family sayings
❏ Favorite proverbs
❏ Favorite memories from the past year
❏ Then-and-now story comparing your family now and ten or twenty or fifty years ago
❏ Family members' holiday memories

Record keeping

❏ E-mail addresses
❏ Requests for e-mail addresses
❏ Address changes
❏ Fax numbers
❏ Work phone numbers
❏ Home phone numbers
❏ Lost relatives

Requests and lists

❏ Requests for news items
❏ List of items available for barter or exchange
❏ Requests for photos (holidays, school holidays, birthdays, vacations)
❏ Surveys
❏ Deadlines for contributing to next issue

Important dates
(see list for family calendars on page 50)

Fun and entertainment

❏ Crossword puzzle with family related clues
❏ Home or family remedies

❑ Jokes
❑ Recipes
❑ Children's drawings
❑ Parenting tips

Reunions (see also Genealogy)

Newsletters have lots of room for the type of details needed to draw members to family reunions. For further information on reunion communications and planning, read *The Family Reunion Handbook* by Tom Ninkovich, listed in the Publishing Tools section on page 104.

On the flip side, reunions are great places to gather stories and information on family members for the newsletter. (See interview questions on pages 86 to 87.)

Have teenagers interview elders and elders interview teenagers.

Reunion news and facts

❑ Time, date and location of the reunion
❑ Return address and phone number
❑ Registration fees
❑ Registration form
❑ Advance registration incentives
❑ Payment procedure
❑ Pet policy
❑ Lodging options
❑ Cancellation policy and refunding rules
❑ Location map and driving instructions
❑ What to bring
❑ Type of weather to expect
❑ What to wear
❑ List of those planning to attend
❑ Schedule or description of program/events

Reunion background information

❑ List of committee members
❑ Phone numbers of committee members
❑ Short history of decisions made and those in progress
❑ Request suggestions for program ideas, award categories and prizes
❑ List volunteer positions
❑ Request information on missing families or family members
❑ Request memorabilia
❑ Family survey
❑ Committee for next year
❑ Next reunion site and information

🐞 🐞 🐞

"After a year and one half of trying to determine where to settle now that I've retired, we decided to return to the Denver area to more fully share in the most precious benefits of our lives: being near our children and grandchildren and reconnecting with many close friends. We have lived over much of the country during our corporate life and have come to realize that our children missed the opportunity to truly know and enjoy their grandparents. We can now give that experience to our grandchildren and at the same time reap more fulfilling lives ourselves."

—John

Reunion warm-ups (news that helps people connect ahead of time)

❑ Recalls of reunions of years past
❑ Reunion trivia
❑ Who was at the last reunion and what are their relations?
❑ News of family not able to attend the reunion
❑ New additions to the family
❑ Memories of a family member who has passed away
❑ Scholarship and family funds
❑ Recipe books
❑ Requests for recipes
❑ Jokes, cartoons
❑ Historical family data
❑ Profiles of family members (maybe a matriarch or patriarch)
❑ Profiles of less well-known members of the family
❑ Who should be thanked for hard work or accomplishments?
❑ Has the family unofficially "adopted" anyone who is now included in family events? Who is the person? How did he or she come to be included? Interview the person about memories of the family.
❑ Ask spouses of family members for their first impressions of the family and how those may have changed over the years.
❑ How was the reunion site chosen?
❑ What wisdom, knowledge or skills have been passed down the generations?
❑ What are some memorable events from the last reunion?
❑ Ask people their earliest memories of reunions.
❑ What family stories get told at every event?
❑ What member of the family is known for telling stories? For telling jokes?
❑ What foods are included at every event? Who makes them?
❑ Print a recipe of an important family food (if the chef is willing to tell).
❑ What keepsakes or mementos have been in the family for many years?
❑ Does anyone have an unusual hobby, job or pet?
❑ Who within the family has the most children?
❑ Who are the oldest and youngest members of the family?
❑ List classifieds—family collection items/swaps.
❑ Family trivia:
   what does the family name mean?
   what language does it come from?
   famous family members
   oldest member
   newest member
   interesting hobbies
   most unusual job
   most kids

Genealogy

Historical information

❑ Family history
❑ Queries about ancestors
❑ Items of family history, past
❑ Bible records
❑ Census records
❑ Genealogy charts, lineages, branches
❑ News of historic family dwellings
❑ Photos of historic dwellings
❑ Photos of historic family members
❑ Family crest
❑ Family credo or motto
❑ Family military history
❑ Stories handed down through generations
❑ Burial and cemetery information
❑ Old, historic wills
❑ Old family letters
❑ Portions of family trees
❑ Offers of printouts of entire family trees
❑ Family physical trait descriptions
❑ Queries about heirlooms
❑ Origination of the family name
❑ What the family name means
❑ Famous members of the family
❑ Interesting, perhaps eccentric, ancestors
❑ Photos of places with family name in the name
❑ Old newspaper clippings
❑ Biographical sketches of relatives (living or deceased)

News from living relatives

❑ Queries about current relatives
❑ Items of family history
❑ Editorials
❑ News from family abroad
❑ Recent deaths
❑ Recent weddings
❑ Recent birth notices
❑ Awards that family members get
❑ Plans for family reunions
❑ Reunion information
❑ Reports on past reunions
❑ Maps to reunion locations or historic family sites

❦ ❦ ❦

"We'd forgotten the joys a newborn brings—the socks so tiny they get stuck in with the dryer lint, the joy of the first smile, the miracle of miniature hands. What the second child really did is make us realize how unnecessarily complicated we'd made things with the first. The most amazing thing about a newborn is that you can set them down and they don't move! On the other hand, nobody mentioned that the quantity of laundry increases exponentially with each being added to a household."

—**Elaine**

❦ ❦ ❦

"My favorite line from Aaron this year was when I asked him to look out the window of our new house at the leaves falling like snow from the trees. He giggled and looked up at me and said, 'Oh Mom, never get caught in a leaf pile with a wet sucker!'"

—**Lori**

❏ Family dwellings for sale
❏ Profiles of current family members
❏ Regional information

Family association news

❏ Updates from the association officers
❏ Board members' listing for family association
❏ Thank you's/recognition for board members' services
❏ Board positions open, qualifications needed, how to apply
❏ General meeting notes
❏ Future meeting announcements

General newsletter items

❏ ISSN# (International Standard Serial Number—if you register your newsletter with the Library of Congress at the National Serials Data Program, Washington, DC 20540)
❏ Index of back issues and how to receive
❏ List of every place where back issues are available
❏ Readership surveys
❏ Subscription information
❏ Requests for money or equipment donations
❏ Information on how to submit articles or queries
❏ Web site addresses for genealogy or family information
❏ E-mail addresses for family members

School News

❏ News from each of the classrooms (or grades)
❏ Editorials
❏ Advice column
❏ Movie reviews
❏ Kids in the news
❏ Calendar of events
❏ Teacher columns
❏ Message from the principal
❏ Club and sports news
❏ Community events or issues
❏ Jokes
❏ Trivia
❏ Classifieds
❏ Time management and stress tips for kids
❏ Study skills tips
❏ Library updates
❏ Internet sites of interest
❏ School mission statement

☙ ☙ ☙

"A lady in Switzerland found out the identity of her father. Her mother would have been a wartime bride if he hadn't been killed on a mission."

— **L. Ray Sears**

Give your roving school reporters press badges.

Wedding

❏ How did the bride and groom meet?

❏ What happened the first time each met the other's parents?

❏ How did he (or she) propose?

❏ How does the groom know the best man?

❏ How does the bride know the maid(en) of honor?

❏ Where are they going on their honeymoon?

❏ Ask the couple what they imagine their lives will be like in five, ten, twenty or fifty years.

❏ Ask them (separately) for favorite names for children and compare the lists.

❏ What is the significance behind the wedding colors?

❏ Are there any unsung heroes of the wedding?

❏ Are there any stories of fun fiascos?

❏ Who traveled the furthest?

❏ What personal touches were added to the ceremony and why?

❏ Who are the other members of the wedding party? How are they related to the bride or groom?

Significant Birthday Newsletters

❏ Famous events that occurred on the same day

❏ Famous people born on that day

❏ Technological advances that have occurred during the person's life

❏ A timeline of the person's life

❏ Who should portray the person in a film about his or her life?

❏ Nicknames the person had

❏ What the person was like as a child; as a teenager

❏ Activities in which he or she participated in school

❏ Interview childhood friends for their impressions of the person

---

❦ ❦ ❦

"Whatever happened to the old-fashioned Christmas? You know. The one from Dickens where you knock off early from work on Christmas Eve, stop on your way home and do your shopping on Main Street. Then, enjoy a warm, happy few days with your family.

Fighting for a parking space at Target doesn't give me the 'Dickens feeling.' Neither does dodging strollers at the mall. Calling 800 numbers for gifts? Packing boxes and waiting in line at UPS? Nope, too much like my day job.

Writing this newsletter does. So we'll see you again here next year."

—Elaine

Interview Questions

The best way to profile a family member in a newsletter is to interview the person. Select questions from the following lists. Transfer the questions to the worksheet on page 89 and use it for the interview.

If you're stuck on writing your own newsletter, look through the following questions, especially "Reviving memories."

Reviving memories (recent and not so recent)

❑ What is your favorite family memory from last year?

❑ What are the high points from last year?

❑ What was your biggest fiasco?

❑ What are you most thankful for?

❑ What was the happiest moment or time period of your life?

❑ What is your biggest regret?

❑ What was your best vacation ever and why?

❑ What is your most treasured memory?

❑ What is the greatest accomplishment of your life? Is there anything you hope to do that is even better?

❑ For what in your life do you feel most grateful?

❑ Was there ever a random or fluke event that dramatically changed the course of your life?

❑ Since being a teenager, in what three-year period has your life changed the most?

❑ Who has been your friend for the longest time? What is special about this person?

❑ What was your first job? (If it's been awhile, how much did you make an hour?)

❑ What was your favorite job and least favorite job?

Writing current news

❑ What are your children's favorite subjects in school?

❑ Which extracurricular activities are they drawn to?

❑ What is your favorite part of your job?

❑ What would you like to be doing more of?

❑ Have you done any home improvement projects?

Getting to know someone

❑ What do you do to relax?

❑ Who is/was your favorite teacher?

❑ What is/was your favorite subject?

❑ Who has influenced you most?

❑ If you could have lunch with anyone (alive or deceased) who would it be and why?

❑ Who are your heroes?

❑ What is your favorite movie of all time?

- What is your favorite book?
- What is your favorite TV show?
- What is your hobby?
- What is your favorite sport to watch and why?
- What is your favorite sport to play and why?
- When is your birthday?
- Where would you like to travel to?
- How do you want to be remembered?
- Whom do you admire most and in what way does that person inspire you?
- If you could wake up tomorrow having gained any one ability or quality, what would it be?
- Your houses catches fire, after saving your loved ones and pets, you can only save one thing, what would it be?
- Would you like to be famous? In what way?
- Is there something you've dreamed of doing for a long time? Why haven't you done it?
- What do you most strive for in your life—accomplishment, security, love, power, excitement, knowledge or something else?
- You win a major award. Which family member do you thank in your acceptance speech?
- If you could take a one-month trip to anywhere in the world and money were not a consideration, where would you go and what would you do?
- If you could have free unlimited service for five years from an extremely good cook, chauffeur, housekeeper, masseuse, or personal secretary, which would you choose?
- What is your typical day like?
- What kind of books do you like to read? What was the last book you read?

For more great interview questions, see *The Book of Questions*, by Gregory Stock and published by Workman Publishing.

Interviewing kids
- What holidays, events or parties are you looking forward to?
- What's your favorite TV program?
- What's your favorite movie?
- What's your favorite song?
- What's your favorite snack?
- What's your favorite sport or game?
- How are your grades?
- Complete this sentence: I can't wait to be _____ years old because I'm going to _____.

Help Me with My Newsletter

Stuck on what to write about? Make this a group project. Hand this worksheet to a friend and discuss the following questions.

What did I do that you found the most interesting?

_____

_____

_____

What was I the most excited about?

_____

_____

_____

What did I complain about the most?

_____

_____

_____

What were the high points of my year?

_____

_____

_____

What were the low points?

_____

_____

_____

What seemed to be the projects that pushed me forward?

_____

_____

_____

Other notes:

_____

_____

_____

Interview Form

Reporter Name:_____

Article Title or Idea: _____

Date of Interview:_____

Spelling of name: _____

Nickname: _____

Family relation: _____

Phone number:_____

Address:_____

Would you like additional copies of the newsletter? How many?:_____

Is a photo available (if you use photos in the newsletter)?:_____

☐ Check here if the person being interviewed asks to approve the article before it's printed.

Question #1: _____

Answer: _____

_____

Question #2: _____

Answer: _____

_____

Question #3: _____

Answer: _____

_____

Question #4: _____

Answer: _____

_____

Question #5: _____

Answer: _____

_____

Question #6: _____

Answer: _____

Tips for Getting Contributions

A very common scenario with family publications is that, while there's much initial enthusiasm for the newsletter project, most family members don't participate in keeping the publication going by contributing articles. Here are some tips to make the newsletter fun for everyone.

❑ Before committing to doing a newsletter, find at last two, preferably three, family members who are willing and able to write a section or two of the newsletter.

❑ Ask people to contribute in different ways, not just writing articles. Ask for photographs, recipes, artwork, cartoons or anything else someone wants to contribute.

❑ Request that articles and information be sent by e-mail or on disk (that way, they're already typed in).

❑ Set early deadlines giving yourself plenty of time for production.

❑ Design a template that can expand or contract as information is available (e-mail and Web sites are great for this).

❑ Let people know that their contributions may be edited for grammar, style and length.

Top 10 Tips for Newsletter Success

These ten tips are from Lisa Suarez Johnson, Editor, *It's All Relative*. Lisa has successfully launched and continued a family newsletter by implementing the following ideas.

1. Determine interest and encourage all readers to participate. Greater involvement means less work for you.

2. Set up a publication schedule so your newsletter is predictable. As the publication date nears, your readers will anticipate the newsletter every time they check their mailboxes!

3. You don't need a professional graphic designer, but it helps to have someone with a good eye for design. Good design invites readership.

4. Attention to detail is a key element. Carefully proofread names, dates, addresses, grammar, spelling, and other details.

5. Personal anecdotes, favorite family recipes, children's artwork, jokes, inspirational quotes, poems, birth and wedding announcements, vacation stories, family updates, and anything from the children...all make for great newsletter reading.

6. Clip art, children's art work and photos all add interest to your newsletter. Use themes, contests, puzzles to generate involvement from readers. Be creative and have fun.

7. Be sure to seek permission and cite your sources for any copyrighted articles you might want to use. When in doubt, leave it out.

8. Include a list of birthdays and other special events. Everyone likes to be remembered on special days.

9. Request donations from readers for postage and printing costs.

10. Keep your newsletter fun, informative and easy to read. Your readers will love you!

Photo Submission Form

Name of person submitting the photo:_____

Phone number: _____

Address, City, State and Zip: _____

Would you like additional copies of the newsletter? How many?:_____

Do you want this photo returned?_____

Names of the people in the photograph: _____

_____

Nickname(s): _____

_____

Family relation(s):_____

_____

Where and when was the picture taken?

_____

_____

What happened right before or right afterwards?

_____

_____

What's going on outside of the frame?

_____

_____

Why does this moment capture the essence of the event?

_____

_____

Other information about the photo?

_____

_____

Reporter Form

Use this form to submit your news to the family newsletter.

Newsletter: _____

Issue/Date: _____

Reporter Name: _____

Phone #: _____

Story Idea or Title: _____

_____

Who is involved/invited: _____

_____

_____

What is the event: _____

_____

_____

When did it (will it) happen: _____

_____

_____

Where: _____

_____

_____

Why did it (will it) happen: _____

_____

_____

How did it happen: _____

_____

_____

Other details: _____

_____

_____

Other people to contact: _____

_____

_____

NewsTools: Writing Tools

Formulas for Letter Openings and Closings

Openings

- ❏ Dear friends
- ❏ Dear family and friends
- ❏ Happy holidays to all
- ❏ Dear Yuletide readers
- ❏ Dear cousins
- ❏ Greetings to all of our friends and loved ones
- ❏ Seasons greetings y'all!
- ❏ Seasons greetings to all of our friends and loved ones
- ❏ New Year's greetings
- ❏ Hello!
- ❏ Hello and happy holidays!
- ❏ "Merry Christmas to all, and to all a good night"
- ❏ "I'm dreaming of a white Christmas"
- ❏ Greetings
- ❏ Happy Holidays
- ❏ Seasons Greetings

Closings

- ❏ Our friends and family are always in our thoughts.
- ❏ We wish you a wonderful new year filled with all that will bring you joy.
- ❏ Merry Christmas to all and to all a good night.
- ❏ Our most sincere wishes go out to all of you for peace, health and serenity in the coming year.
- ❏ I hope this card finds you and your family in good health and happiness. Keep in touch and stay wonderful.
- ❏ In this season of new life, we wish you and your growing families a happy and safe holiday season.

> "To send a letter is a good way to go somewhere without moving anything but your heart."
> **—Phyllis Theroux**
> *House Beautiful*

> "Though my own life is filled with activity, letters encourage momentary escape into other's lives and I come back to my own with greater contentment."
> **—Elizabeth Forsythe Hailey**
> *A Woman of Independent Means*

Theme headings for the holidays

❑ Joy to the world

❑ You better watch out, you better not cry

❑ Silent night, holy night

❑ Silver bells, silver bells

❑ We wish you a Merry Christmas

Newsletter Names

Here are some sample names from family publications. Notice how many use the family name followed by a news-oriented word that begins with the same letter. For example, my newsletter could be *The Floyd Files* or the *Floyd Front Porch*. Use the alphabetical listing starting on the next page to do the same for your own publication. Have fun!

Adams Family

Ayars Heirs

Bell Chimes

Bird Branches

Born Young Newsletter
    for the Young family

Burton Bits 'N' Business

Butcher Block

Carpenter Chronicles

The News-Caster
    for the Castor family

Chamberlain Chain

Chilson Chatter

Coffey Cousins' Clearinghouse

Diggin' for Davises

Discovering Denny Descendants

Fine Lines

Fore Front

Foust Family Forum

The Garrison Gazette

Getting Gray

Golding Nuggets

Handwriting on the Walls
    for the Wall family

Hottenstein Lines

Keener Kinfolk

Keeping Up with the Joneses

Le Despencer
    for the Spencer family

The Lemmon Tree

Love Letters

Linn Lineage

Marney Monitor

Mefford Memories

Mendenhall Matters

Norton Notes

Packard's Progress

Pages from the Past

Patterson People

Radford Ramblings

Ragsdale Register

Ransom Researcher
    [Ed.: What about Ransom Notes?]

Romig Reflections

Sanders Siftings

The Shepherd Flock

The Shore Line

Stanford Sagas

Stanley Stepping Stones

Taft Tree Talk

Terrell Trails

Tiner Times

Tracing Turner

Waller Wanderings

Wheeler Writings

The Widdows Web

Wandering Wolfs

Yates of Yore

❦ ❦ ❦

Joy to the world... Yes it is that time of year. I usually reserve this phrase until the end of May when I see three months of vegetation and total bliss ahead of me. However, through Ben's eyes I have been able to look beyond Target's parking lot and see the joy in the season. I hope this card and letter finds everyone reflecting on a wonderful year and looking forward to a new one.

You better watch out, you better not cry... Of course, I am referring to my reaction to Ben starting not only day care this year, but also pre-school....

A

about …
abstract
accolades
accomplishments
achievers
advocate
agenda
alert
ambassador
ancestry
announcement
announcer
answer
anthem
applause

B

banner
beacon
beat
bell
benefactor
best
blabber/blurt
blessings
blueprint
booster
branches
bridge
briefings
briefs
broadcast
bugle
bulletin
bullhorn
business
buzz
by-lines

C

cable
calendar
calling…
calling card
… calls
capsule
chain
champion
channel
charter
chat
chatter

chime
chorus
chronicle
circuit
citizen
classified(s)
clearinghouse
clips
coalition
collection(s)
column
comments
communicator
communique
companion
compass
compendium
connection(s)
contemplations
conversations
copy
corner
council
courier
cousins
credits
creed
crossings
crusader
currents

D

data
dateline
declarations
delicacies
depot
descendants
destination(s)
dialog
digest
diggings
directions
discovering…
discussion
dispatch
distinctions
doings
doorways
doubletakes
dreams
dwellings

E

ear
echo
emblem
enterprises
enthusiast
envoy
epigram/epigraph
essence
essentials
etc.
events
examiner
examples
excellence
excerpts
exchange(s)
exclamations
experience
explorer
expressions
extra
eye

F

facets
facts
faithful
family
family corners
family ties
FAQs
favorites
feedback
fellowship
files
findings
…first
flash
flock
flyer
focus
fold
folklore
folks
footprints
footsteps
forefront
foreword
forum
411 (younger audiences)
friend(s)
front, front line

front porch
future
FYI

G

gab
gallery
galore
gateways
gathering
gazette
gems
generations
gifts
globe
glory
goings on
grab bag
…gram
grassroots
greetings
group
growth
guardian
guide

H

handwriting
happenings
harbor
harvest
headlines
headstart
herald
heritage
highlights
highways
hints
historical review
history
hodgepodge
holdings (financial, real estate)
homepage
homespun …
horizons
hotline
hullabaloo
hunters
hunting…

I

ideas
illumination

images
impact
impressions
imprint
in brief
information
informer
ink
inklings
inquiries
inside/insider
insights
issues
items
itinerary

J

jargon
joiner
jottings
journal
journeys
jubilee
junctions

K

keepers
keeping up with …
keepsake
kernels
key
keynotes
keystone
kibitzer
kin
kinfolk
kith and kin
kudos

L

leader
leaflet
letter(s)
levity
lineage
lines
lingo
linkages
linking…
links
list(s)
listing(s)
litany

look-out
loop

M

magic
mailer
mantra
map
mastermind
matters
matters of fact
meanderings
members
memo
memories
mentions
mentor
message
messenger
milestones
miracles
mission
monitor
monthly
morsels
mysteries

N

narrator
navigator
neighbor
network
news
news brief
newsline
newsworthy…
notables
notes
noteworthy…
notice
now
nuts & bolts

O

oasis
observer
occasions
odds & ends
offbeat
offline
online
opportunities
orbits

outlook
outreach
out-write
ovation
overture
overview

P

page
pandemonium
panorama
papers
partners
passages
passing notes
passport
passwords
pastures
pathways
peeks/peaks
peers
pennant
people
perspective
peruser
pilot
planner
platform
pointers
pontifications
postmarks
potluck
potpourri
press
pride
profile
progress
prolific
prose
prospectus
proverbs
pulse
pursuit(s)

Q

Q&A
quarterly
query
quest
quick takes
quill
quips
quotes

R

rabbit ears
radio
ramblings
rapport
reader
readings
read me
recipe
records
reflections
refrains
register
relay
release
reminder
report
reporter
researcher
resource
reunion
review(s)
…in review
roll call
roots
roster
roundup
route
rumors
the rundown
Rx

S

safari
sagas
salute
sanctuary
satellite
scene
scholar
scoop
scope
scout
scuttlebutt
searcher
searching…
secrets
seeking…
sentinel
settlements
sheet
shenanigans
shepherd

shindig
shorts
siftings
signal
signature
sketches
skimmings
smalltalk
smiles
snapshots
society
soundings
source
speaking of…
speaks
spectrum
spin
spinoff
spirit
splash
spotlight
stats
stepping stones
story/stories
straight talk
summary
summit
sundries
supplement
supporter
surveyor
synopsis

T

takes
taking stock
talents
tales
talk
tangents
tattler
team
tempo
testament
thoughts
threads
tidbits
tidings
ties
times
tip off
tips
to-and-fro

toasts
today
tokens
tracing…
trails
traveler
treasures
tree
trends
tributaries
trifles
tunes
twist

U
unifier
uniter
update
upfront
uplift
uplink
ups and downs
upstart
upswing
uptake
up-to-date

V
value(s)
vantage
variety
ventures
verbatim
vernacular
verses
viewpoint
views
vignette(s)
villager
vim & vigor
vine
visible
vision
visionary
vistas
viva …
voice
volume
volunteer

W
wagon

wandering(s)
watch
watchers
watering hole
wave
way
web
welcome
whims
whispers
whoopee
who's who
window
wire
wisdom
wish list
wishing well
wit
wit & wisdom
wonders
word
word for word
world
worldwide
wrap-up
write-up
writings

X
x-ray

Y
yak
yearnings
yields
yippee
of yore

Z
zeal
zest
zone
zoom

Headings for Standing Columns

Some family newsletters have special sections—for news, family profiles, jokes and so on. For the headings of these sections, here are some ideas.

News
What's New?
In the News
Top of the News
Did You Know?
Did You Hear?
The Newsdesk
Tell Me More
The Latest News
At a Glance
Check It Out
What's Up?
Hot Off the Presses
Stop the Presses
The Toolbox
Readables
Notables
The Round Table
Heads Up
News and Notes
New and Noteworthy
For the Record
Facts and Footnotes
In the Spotlight
In Brief
Highlights
News and Views
Tidbits
Bits and Pieces
Bits-n-Pieces
Bits and Bytes
The Nitty-Gritty
Much Ado About Something
Nuts-n-Bolts
Updates
That's Good to Know
News, Views, Reviews, To-do's
Resources
On the Record
Checkmarks
Hotline
Fit to Print
FYI
Get the Scoop
What-Nots
What's New With You?
What's Notable?
What's the Good Word?

Family Profiles
What's the Buzz?
What's the Scoop?

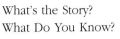

What's the Story?
What Do You Know?
What's all the Hubbub, Bub?
Star Performers
In the Spotlight
In the Limelight
Curtain Calls
Bursting With Pride
Our Pride and Joy
The Center of Attention
Behind the Scenes
Standing Ovations
Bravo!
Making a Name
Introducing ...
Meet 'Em and Greet 'Em
Putting a Face With a Name
Where Credit is Due
You're the Tops
Apples of Our Eye
Praiseworthy
Honorable Mentions
People, Places and Things
From the Grapevine
News from the Pews

Letters
Feedback
Letter Perfect
Verbatim
Mailbag
Mailbox
Postmarks
From the Grapevine
Pass Us a Note
Reader Round Table
What's on Your Mind?
The Suggestion Card
Your Turn

Background Information
Queries
Questions and answers
Q&A
FAQs (Frequently Asked Questions)
Asked & Answered
You've Been Asking
We Want to Know
You Want to Know
Information, Please
Since You Asked
The Sounding Board

Editorials
On My Mind
In My Opinion
In My View
News from...
[name] Says ...
Take It From Me
A Letter From [name]
From the Soapbox
From [name's] Keyboard
Welcome from [name]
Sage Advice
Memo from [name]
Greetings and Salutations
Editorial Echoes
Editorial Ear
Editorial Eye
Editorial Expressions
The Op-Ed Section
Perspectives
Insights

Events
What's Happening?
What's Going On?
What's Up Doc?
What's Up?
What's Next?

Calendars
Wonderings and Wanderings
Goings On
Get Up and Go
Around Town
Reminders
Countdown to ...

Entertainment
What's Been Said?
What's Wise?
What's My Line?
What's Funny?
What's Inspiring?
What If?
What's Worth Repeating?
What's the Answer?
What's Cookin'?
Fun Facts
Sound Bites
Quotable Quotes
Did You Know?
What's the Answer?

The Top 10 Reasons
Brain Teasers
Food for Thought

Incentives
What's the Deal?
What's In It For You?
Quick Reply
You Asked For It, You Got It
Freebies
Check Out Our Web Site at
(www.whatever.com)
From Our Family to Yours
Opportunity Knocks
Wish List

Writing Worksheet

For most family newsletters, your written story should sound as if you're telling it to a friend. Follow these planning steps for your most important news stories.

❏ What are the three most important, unique, interesting or significant aspects of this story? Include what makes it memorable, why it should be told and why readers should want to read it. The answers to these questions can give you the lead or introduction to your story and keep the story focused.

1. _____

2. _____

3. _____

❏ Answer the five W's and an H for your story:

1. Who? _____

2. What? _____

3. When? _____

4. Where? _____

5. Why? _____

6. How? _____

❏ List the details that can help you bring the story to life. (This avoids vague words like "nice" or "beautiful.") What sensory words can you use to describe the event?

1. Sight _____

2. Sound _____

3. Touch _____

4. Taste _____

5. Smell _____

❏ What quotes can you add from people involved in the story?

_____

❏ What background information could you include?

_____

❏ Think about the emotional aspect of your story to set the tone for your writing. Do you want it to be touching, humorous, straightforward, nostalgic, light or serious? _____

Editing Worksheet

Once you've written your draft, look at the article using these six steps.

1. Where is detail missing from your story?

2. Where can you add concrete words and sensory descriptions?

3. Where can you make your writing more conversational? Have you used contractions ("it's" instead of "it is") to keep your writing informal? Have you used pronouns ("I" and "you") to keep the writing light and personal?

4. If the story seems too short, it's probably fine. You may have already said everything that needed to be said.

5. If the story is too long (a more common occurrence), ask yourself these questions:

   ❏ What unnecessary words can you remove? For example, replace "at the present time" with "now." "The 1999 Annual Smith Family reunion" could be replaced with "This year's reunion"; the rest is implied.

   ❏ What unnecessary detail have you added? Detail is good, but irrelevant detail can be distracting. Telling readers about your room addition is interesting, but they probably don't need to know the color of the carpet and wallpaper, and they definitely don't want to know how much you spent.

   ❏ Have you taken on too much territory? Maybe you've tried to combine two stories into one. Maybe the annual overview should be split into seasons.

6. As a test for what's important in a story, have someone else read your first draft, then set it aside. Ask your reader what he or she remembers about your story. This will tell you what details stand out. Ask if the reader had any questions. This will point out any missing information.

Teaching Tools

The following are some ways, separated by age group, to involve kids with newsletters either in the classroom or at home.

Preschool and Kindergarten

❏ Focus more on drawings than words.

❏ Have kids dictate the news and teachers or parents can write.

❏ Have children make a vacation newsletter at the start of the school year.

❏ Teachers can use a monthly newsletter to keep parents informed.

❏ If the school has computers, students can use kid-friendly software to write and illustrate stories that can be compiled into a newsletter.

Grade School

❏ Each student can do a summer or vacation newsletter at the beginning of the year.

❏ The class can do a newsletter after a field trip.

❏ Students can use computers to write and illustrate stories.

❏ Each student or the whole class can do a class newsletter before an open house or parent-teacher conference.

❏ Newsletters can combine activities from writing classes, art classes and computer classes for cross-disciplinary benefits.

❏ Newsletters can be a monthly or bi-monthly project to create class history and archives.

Junior High and High School

❏ Newsletter projects can work in conjunction with yearbook projects.

❏ Photography classes can work with English or computer classes to produce a school newsletter.

❏ Clubs and teams can do newsletters to keep the rest of the school informed and promote the group's activities.

❏ If the school is online, students can create a Web site newsletter and learn electronic publishing.

❏ Each grade can put out a newsletter to keep parents and students informed about meetings, dances, sporting events, etc.

NewsTools:
Publishing Tools

Ways to Stretch Your Budget

Here are some general money-saving suggestions followed by other tips from the pros.

❑ Limit your list.

❑ Send the newsletter by e-mail.

❑ Publish photos on your family Web site.

❑ Distribute to family hubs—then it's their job to duplicate or pass along.

❑ Shop around for office supplies. —Richard G. Boyd

❑ Keep the format simple. —Patrick Demuth

❑ If it costs more than 32 cents to mail your newsletter, send complimentary sample pages to prospective subscribers. —Jeff Linscott

❑ Learn to do as much layout and production work as you can. Buy a scanner to copy text and photos. Don't be afraid to ask questions about how to do processes at the photocopy shop. —Cynthia L. Leet

❑ Use 11 x 17 paper and mail it yourself. —L. Ray Sears

❑ Copy yourself via your own copy machine. —Carolyn Weidner

❑ Printing costs are discounted by volume. It may pay for you to print more copies and donate the extras to libraries and hold some to sell as sample copies. —Lynne D. Miller

❑ Get your family association chartered as an IRS Not-for-Profit organization. Do not claim that everyone of the surname is related. —Larry Hamilton

❑ Everytime you go to press, check every copy house in town. Prices change all of the time. The one I use now got tired of losing me so she agreed to do my printing for 3 cents per page, period. —Jo Havens

Ways to Fund the Newsletter

❑ Ask family members to send stamps.

❑ Ask families to subscribe or send donations.

❑ Alternate families to underwrite the costs for an entire year or issue and credit "this issue is brought to you by …"

> ❧ ❧ ❧
>
> "I played with the title page especially, also the borders, how the photos were laid out and the total number of pages, so as to get the best value for postage. I have since decided on 18 printed pages—this, with an envelope, costs 78¢ to mail, whereas 20 pages is right on the borderline for $1.01."
>
> — **Jeff**

Books on Family

Family Reunion Handbook
by Tom Ninkovich
Reunion Research
3145 Geary Blvd. #14
San Francisco, CA 94118
(209) 855-2101

Reunion Research also offers books, games, mailing supplies and other resources for reunion planners.

Family Traditions
by Elizabeth Berg
Readers Digest Books

The 7 Habits of Highly Effective Families
by Stephen R. Covey
Golden Books
888 Seventh Ave.
New York, NY 10106

Books on Newsletters and Publishing

Desktop Publishing & Design for Dummies
by Roger C. Parker
IDG Books Worldwide, Inc.
919 E. Hillsdale Blvd., Ste. 400
Foster City, CA 94404
(800) 434-3422

Home Sweet Home Page
by Robin Williams
Peachpit Press
2414 Sixth Street
Berkeley, CA 94710
(510) 548-4393
www.peachpit.com/home-sweet-home

Kids in Print
by Mark Levin
Good Apple, Simon & Schuster
299 Jefferson Rd.
Parsippany, NJ 07054-0480

The Newsletter Editor's Handbook
by Marvin Arth, Helen Ashmore
and Elaine Floyd
Newsletter Resources
6614 Pernod Ave.
St. Louis, MO 63139
(314) 647-0400

The Newsletter Sourcebook
by Mark Beach and Elaine Floyd
North Light Books
1507 Dana Avenue
Cincinnati, OH 45207
(513) 531-2690

Quick & Easy Newsletters
by Elaine Floyd
Newsletter Resources
6614 Pernod Ave.
St. Louis, MO 63139
(314) 647-0400

Books on Crafts and Photography

Creative Rubber Stamping Techniques
by MaryJo McGraw
North Light Books
1507 Dana Avenue
Cincinnati, OH 45207
(513) 531-2690

Creative Techniques for Photographing Children
by Vik Orenstein
Writer's Digest Books
1507 Dana Avenue
Cincinnati, OH 45207
(513) 531-2690

Family Memories
(Preserve Treasured Moments with
Scrapbooks and Memory Albums)
by Suzanne McNeill and Lani Stiles
Betterway Books
1507 Dana Avenue
Cincinnati, OH 45207
(513) 531-2690

How to Fold, *editions 1 and 2*
by Larry Withers
Art Direction Book Company
10 E. 39th St.
New York, NY 10016
(212) 889-6500

Make Cards!
(Art & Activities for Kids)
by Kim Solga
North Light Books
1507 Dana Avenue
Cincinnati, OH 45207
(513) 531-2690

**World's Best & Easiest Photography
Book**
by Jerry Hughes
Phillips Lane Publishing
5521 Greenville Ave., Ste. 104-732
Dallas, TX 75206

Genealogy Resources

Magazines:

Everton's Genealogical Helper
The Everton Publishers
P.O. Box 368
Logan, UT 84323-0368
(800) 443-6325; (801) 752-6022

Books:

**For all Time: A Complete Guide to
Writing Family History**
by Charley Kempthorne
Heinemann
361 Hanover St.
Portsmouth, NH 03801-3912
(603) 431-7894

**Writing Family Histories and
Memoirs**
by Kirk Polking
Betterway Books
1507 Dana Avenue
Cincinnati, OH 45207
(513) 531-2690

Web Sites:

Cyndi's List of Genealogical Sites
http://www.cyndilist.com

**Family Associations, Newsletters &
Mailing Lists**
http://home.texoma.net/~mmc-
mullen/6doc.htm

Books—Research Preparation
http://www.agll.com/books/resprep.html

Genealogy—from The Mining Co.
http://genealogy.miningco.com

How to Genealogy
http://server.mediasoft.net/ScottC/
  Howto.htm

Genealogy Usenet Newsgroups
http://genealogy.miningco.com/msub24
.htm

**Madigan's Books—Buy and Sell
Books of Genealogical Interest**
http://www.advant.com/madigan
physical adddress: P.O. Box 62
Charleston, IL 61920
(217)345-3657

What's New in Genealogy Pages
http://www.genhomepage.com/whats_
new.html

Clip Art & Templates

Several companies offer large collections of clip art for under $20.00. Larger collections, with over 100,000 images, are available for under $40.00. The better products have a variety of styles of art available — traditional, contemporary, etc. Broderbund offers a collection of holiday and celebration clip art for $29.99. These collections are available on CD-ROM or disk and can be purchased at office supply or computer supply stores or from catalogs.

Tips for Finding Clip Art Online

Strategies vary depending on which search engine you're using. Try putting the words free clip art in quotation marks — "free clip art" — and you should get several good hits immediately. The quotation marks mean that all three words have to appear together, in that order. If there's a specific type of clip art you want, put a plus sign (+) in front of "free clip art" and what you're looking for. For example, you could search for +"free clip art" +Christmas. The plus sign means the word or phrase following must appear in the site.

A lot of clip art can be downloaded or sent to you on disk. Pay attention to the format of the picture. Much of the clip art on the web is designed for use on the Web; these will have .gif and .jpeg extensions. The ones you'll want for your newsletter will be called .bmp, .pcx, .tif (.tiff or .pict for Macintoshes), etc.

The Web site http://www.desktoppub.tqn.com/mlibrary.htm has links to several companies that offer free clip art online.

Tips for Finding Templates Online

Strategies vary depending on which search engine you're using. Try putting the words newsletter template in quotation marks — "newsletter template." If you don't get the results you want, try separating the words with a plus sign in front of each — +newsletter +template. You can also try the words "creating newsletters" in quotation marks. You could add your software program to the search by entering something like +"creating newsletters" +"Microsoft Word."

The Web site http://www.desktoppub.tqn.com/mlibrary.htm has links to several companies that offer templates listed by software type.

Desktop Publishing Software

For home use, desktop publisher software comes in two categories: lower end but more affordable, and more expensive but more sophisticated. On the more affordable side, many programs are avaible for under $30. With these, users are usually more limited in design and layout choices. The higher end programs usually cost $50 to $100 but allow for more flexibility and a more professional design. For a once-a-year publisher, the lower end programs are fine, if you don't mind the limitations. These are also useful for complete computer novices.

Shop for software at office supply stores, computer supply or software stores or through catalogs or online sources.

❏ Budget Conscious Software
  Print It Plus
  ROM Tech

❏ Publisher 3
  CompuWorks

❏ Greetings Workshop
  Microsoft

❏ Birthday Newsletters
  Expert Software

Higher End Desktop Publisher Software

❏ Microsoft Publisher
  Microsoft

❏ PrintMaster Platinum
  Mindscape

❏ PrintShop Publishing Suite
  Broderbund

❏ Print House
  Corel

Software for Kids

❏ The Amazing Writing Machine & Kid Pix
  Broderbund

❏ Avery Kidshouse Printertainment Software
  Avery Dennison

Software for Calendars and Puzzles

Many desktop publishing programs can produce calendars, but if yours doesn't you can buy a separate program. There are several programs for under $20. Some calendar programs are more like appointment books that let you create a to-do list instead of graphics programs that let you create an attractive and fun calendar for printing.

❏ Custom Calendar
  ROM Tech

❏ Calendar Creator
  Creative Office

❏ Calendar Creator Plus
  SoftKey

❏ Calendar Creator
  The Learning Company

❏ Puzzlemaker
  http://www.puzzlemaker.com

❏ Crossword Construction Kit
  http://www.crossword
  kit.com/index.htm.
  Insight Software Solutions, Inc.
  P.O. Box 354
  Bountiful, UT 84011
  (801) 295-1890

❏ Crossworks
  Homeware
  ttp://www.homeware.com

Software for Photo Editing

Computer Software:

Good programs to try are Adobe Photoshop, Microsoft Photo Editor and Corel Photo.

CD-ROM Photos:

Your local photo developer may be able to transfer your pictures to CD-ROM.

Web site:

Family Dimensions (http://www.cyber-pages.com/fotoscan/) specializes in the home and family market and offers scanning of photos and documents onto CD.

Mail Order Catalogs for Software

MicroWarehouse (for PCs)
(800) 367-6808

MacWarehouse (for Macintoshes)
(800) 622-6222

Pre-Printed Newsletter Papers

Check your local office supply stores, card shops and stationery stores for other papers. Kinko's and other copying service stores also offer pre-printed papers for newsletters. Or call or write for a catalog from these companies:

Great Papers
2080 Lookout Drive
North Mankato, MN 56003
(507) 386-1044

Paper Direct
P.O. Box 1514
Secaucus, NJ 07096
(800) 272-7377

The Web site http://www.desktoppub.tqn.com/-mlibrary.htm has links to several companies that offer newsletter and other specialty stationery.

Low-Cost Color Copies by Mail Order

If you want to photocopy your newsletter in color, first call your local copy shops and ask for the cost of duplicating the quantity you need. Most prices will be in the range of 79¢ to $1 per page.

Next, search the Web or call the following services that we found by searching for "best prices for color photocopies." Mail order prices for quantities over 50 averaged 75¢. For over 100, the prices dropped to 49¢.

Express Digital Images
(800) 283-6556
http://www.expressdigitalimages.com

Sterling Copy Center, Inc.
(800) 787-8375
http://www.colorcopies.com

Colorama
(800) 714-4445
http://www.color-copies.com

Copy-Ready Templates for Your Newsletter

The following pages are set up for you to photocopy the templates and use for your own newsletters. For best use, use the reduce and enlarge feature on your photocopier to create the image in the desired size. Mix and match the images to create an original design. Have fun!

Last Year's Keepsakes And Memories

Favorite Facts

What's your favorite food?

_____

What's your favorite dessert?

_____

If you could go anywhere on vacation, where would you go? What would you do there?

What's your favorite subject in school?

_____

What's your favorite toy?

_____

Index

Acknowledgements

This project begins and ends at the mailbox. Out of a need to stay connected with my own friends and family who are scattered throughout the world, I started sending newsletters to their mailboxes. The messages back to mine let me know that the newsletter format worked and gave me the idea to do this book. Thank you, my friends.

In the Making...

When I started requesting newsletters for this book, my mailbox was filled with newsletters from other families. From reading the messages—many of them so moving it was hard at times to keep the linear thought process necessary to write—I learned that sharing news works to hold other friends and families together, too. These families not only graciously allowed us to peek into their mailboxes, they've opened their front doors and invited us in. And, for that, I send a heartfelt thanks and wishes for lives filled with millions of joys and smiles.

I'd also like to thank the team that helped put this book together. Newsletter Resources' editorial director, Susan Todd, helped select the newsletters, wrote many of the captions and pulled together much of the NewsTools section. She even enlisted the help of her niece and nephew to test and create the children's activities. Thank you, Sarah and Jonathan.

Original graphics and photographs were created by the ace design team at VIP Graphics. They not only provide beautiful graphical elements and cover photography, they also entertain children and give great backrubs!

Into Your Hands...

You may have heard about this book through articles or mentions in the media. This happened through the hard work of Kate and Doug Bandos of KSB Promotions. Thank you for all of your great ideas and support.

This book got into your hands with the help of the talented distribution team at Writer's Digest Books. Many thanks to Jenny Walsh and David Lewis who first saw the need for this book, and Stacie Berger, Kate DeRosier, Richard Hunt, Liz Koffel, Mert Ransdell, Laura Smith, Budge Wallis, Joanne Widmer and their teams who've put their incredible talents behind promoting it. And special thanks for the support from the quality bookstore, art store or library who has stocked it for your easy access.

And, to all of you reading this book, best wishes for staying in touch with your community of family and friends by sharing your good news.

YOU HAVE MAIL

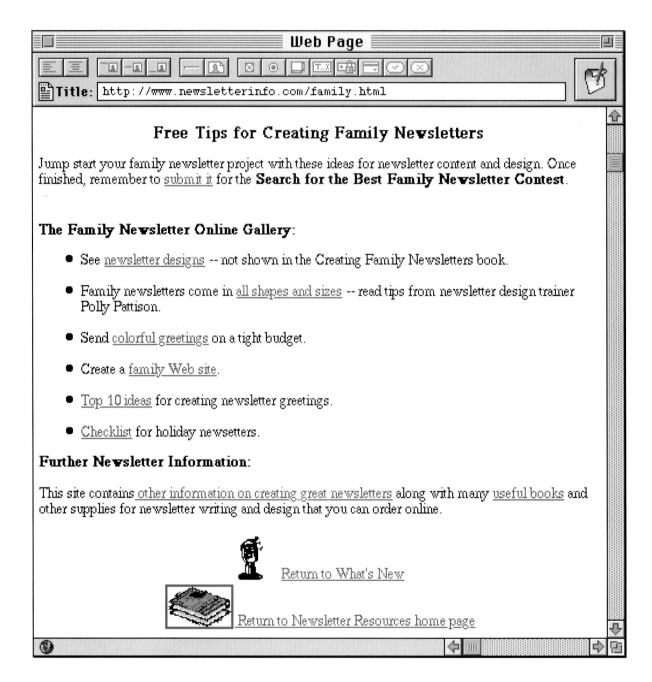

Free Tips for Creating Family Newsletters

Jump start your family newsletter project with these ideas for newsletter content and design. Once finished, remember to submit it for the **Search for the Best Family Newsletter Contest**.

The Family Newsletter Online Gallery:

- See newsletter designs -- not shown in the Creating Family Newsletters book.

- Family newsletters come in all shapes and sizes -- read tips from newsletter design trainer Polly Pattison.

- Send colorful greetings on a tight budget.

- Create a family Web site.

- Top 10 ideas for creating newsletter greetings.

- Checklist for holiday newsetters.

Further Newsletter Information:

This site contains other information on creating great newsletters along with many useful books and other supplies for newsletter writing and design that you can order online.

Return to What's New

Return to Newsletter Resources home page

Visit the Newsletter Resources Site Online

For further tips and information on newsletters, visit the Newsletter Resources site on the Web at http://www.newsletterinfo.com. Or, send a self-addressed, stamped envelope for a free catalog of newsletter books and supplies:

Newsletter Resources
6614 Pernod Ave.
St. Louis, MO 63139